PRESENTED TO:

_____

FROM:

_____

ON THE OCCASION OF:

_____

DECEMBER 31

What are your thoughts as you look back over the last year?
Was it a year of heartache and loss, tragedy and sorrow?
Or happiness and joy, success and achievement?
Do you close the book on this year with regret, or with relief?

No matter what your answer is, I hope you will pause and prayerfully ask yourself two important questions. First, how do you think God looks on this past year in your life? Did it bring you any closer to Him? Second, what lessons will you take from this year into the next? What did God teach you?

Don't be bound by the past and its failures. But don't forget its lessons either.

But one thing I do: Forgetting what is behind and straining toward what is ahead, I press on toward the goal to win the prize for which God has called me heavenward in Christ Jesus.
PHILIPPIANS 3:13–14

Wisdom For Each Day
Billy Graham

Mfd. for © 2011 DaySpring Cards, Inc., Siloam Springs, AR 72761.

Made in China

DECEMBER 30

God is the same yesterday, today, and tomorrow. And because He is unchanging, He is utterly trustworthy and faithful. God is unchanging in His holiness: "Holy, holy, holy is the Lord Almighty!" (Isaiah 6:3).

God is unchanging in His demand for holiness and integrity in our lives: "Consecrate yourselves and be holy, because I am holy" (Leviticus 11:44; 1 Peter 1:15–16).

God is unchanging in His judgment: He will judge all the earth, welcoming some into His eternal presence and sending others to eternal death (Matthew 7:22–23).

God is unchanging in His love: He sent His Son to die on the cross for us sinners.

I the Lord do not change.

MALACHI 3:6

JANUARY 1

[There are] two reasons why it can be good to make resolutions at the beginning of a new year. First, it forces us to look at ourselves—to be honest about our failures and our need to change. The exercise of examining ourselves—with God's help—and seeing where we fall short is important.

Second, making a list of resolutions can turn us to God. If we are honest, we know we fall far short of being what we ought to be—and because of that, we need God's forgiveness. We'll also realize that we can't live the way we should in our own strength. We need God's help.

Give careful thought to your ways.

HAGGAI 1:5

DECEMBER 29

Jesus is the Crucified Christ. Good works won't get us to heaven. Only what Jesus did when He died in our place and shed His blood can open Heaven's door for us.

In addition, Jesus is the Conquering Christ. He rose from the dead as the Conqueror of sin and death and Hell. Because the Risen Jesus holds the keys of hell and death, we don't ever have to experience them for ourselves.

And finally, Jesus is the Coming Christ: Someday He will return to establish His kingdom of peace and blessing.

May your faith and hope be in Christ—today and always!

The Spirit of the Lord is upon Me, because He has anointed Me. To preach the gospel to the poor.

LUKE 4:18 NKJV

JANUARY 2

As we start a new year, the Bible tells us there can be hope for the future.

First, there is hope of a changed person. We are incapable of ridding ourselves of the selfishness and greed that cause conflict and strife and war. Our only hope is a changed heart—and Jesus is in the business of changing hearts.

Second, there is hope of a changed world. When we know Christ, He gives us by His Spirit a new love and concern for others. Changed by Christ, we can begin to change our world.

Third, there is hope of an unchanging eternity in Heaven. This world is not all there is.

If anyone is in Christ, he is a new creation; old things have passed away; behold, all things have become new.

2 CORINTHIANS 5:17 NKJV

DECEMBER 28

In light of these words of John, we should not be surprised that we have four accounts of Jesus' life in the Bible, for each of the four Gospels gives us details about our Lord that are not found in the others.

Never forget: these four accounts of Jesus' life aren't merely interesting stories. Instead, they are accurate, historical accounts of the most important event in human history: the coming of God's Son into the world. Because He came, we can know what God is like. And because He came, we can be saved from our sins. This is good news—which is exactly what the word *gospel* means.

If every one of [the things Jesus did] were written down,
I suppose that even the whole world would not have room
for the books that would be written.

JOHN 21:25

JANUARY 3

God has a plan or purpose for every person, although many people go through life without ever thinking about it. But their lack of awareness doesn't change the fact that God put each of us here for a purpose.

We aren't here by accident. We are here because God put us here. And He put us here for a reason: so we could come to know Him in a personal way and then live in a way that brings glory to His name.

Teach me your way, O Lord; lead me in a straight path.
PSALM 27:11

DECEMBER 27

Christianity has its roots in the deep, firm soil of history. Jesus' incarnation—God invading human history with His presence in the form of man—is on the record. Every time you write the date, you attest to the fact that God entered human history.

Jesus came into the world so we might know that God cares how we live, what we believe, and how we will die. Jesus came to demonstrate to us that we were made to have a personal relationship with God. He came to bridge the gap that separated us from our Creator.

God was reconciling the world to himself in Christ,
not counting men's sins against them.

2 CORINTHIANS 5:19

JANUARY 4

If Christianity is important at all, then it is all-important. If it is anything at all, then it is everything. It is either the most vital thing in your life, or it isn't worth bothering with.

Repent, for the kingdom of heaven is near.

MATTHEW 4:17

DECEMBER 26

In his fear and raging jealousy, King Herod responded to the newborn Jesus with bloodthirsty hostility: "Destroy Him! Let Him die while He is still in His cradle!"

This response grew and swelled until one day many years later it became a mad mob's terrifying roar: "Take him away! Take him away! Crucify him!" (John 19:15).

A reigning Christ, an invading Christ, a revolutionary Christ, a life-changing Christ—that is unacceptable to millions of people. That is a menace to their way of life.

During this Christmas season, however, may you welcome this reigning Christ, invading Christ, revolutionary Christ, life-changing Christ into your life anew.

Then, being divinely warned in a dream that they should not return to Herod, they departed for their own country another way.... Then Herod, when he saw that he was deceived by the wise men, was exceedingly angry.

MATTHEW 2:12, 16 NKJV

JANUARY 5

In what ways might we be like [the man who said he'd rather enjoy his life, even if it shortened his days]? What health rules are we violating?

In what ways are we not taking care of the body God has given us? Someday each one of us who follows Jesus as our Savior and Lord will leave behind our earthly tent—our flesh-and-bone body—and join Him in Heaven for eternity. But until that day—as the Bible says—"Honor God with your body" (1 Corinthians 6:20).

We know that if the earthly tent we live in is destroyed,
we have a building from God, an eternal house in heaven.

2 CORINTHIANS 5:1

DECEMBER 25

It would have been logical to expect God to tear open the
heavens and descend to earth in majesty and power on
that first Christmas night—but He didn't.

Instead, on that quiet night in Bethlehem, a virgin mother laid her
squalling newborn baby into a manger designed to feed cattle.

Truly God works in mysterious ways, His wonders to perform.
The birth of Jesus Christ—the Son of God, our Savior—went unnoticed
by the vast majority of the world that first Christmas night, but no event
in human history was more significant. May His birth—and all it means
—not go unnoticed in our lives!

*So [the shepherds] hurried off and found Mary and Joseph,
and the baby, who was lying in the manger.*

LUKE 2:16

JANUARY 6

In many contexts, VIP means "Very Important Person." But the acronym also offers us a character test. The V stands for VISION, for "where there is no vision, the people perish" (Prov. 29:18, KJV). The letter I stands for INTEGRITY, meaning that a person is the same on the inside as he or she appears on the outside. The P stands for PRESENCE—God's presence in our lives. Without God's help we are doomed. So be steadfast in your commitment to Christ, and be a real VIP—a person with vision, integrity, and God's presence.

Do not conform any longer to the pattern of this world,
but be transformed by the renewing of your mind.

ROMANS 12:2

DECEMBER 24

The first Christmas worship service was conducted not in a temple, a cathedral, or a synagogue, but in the great outdoors. The tidings of Christ's birth echoed in the skies as the angel of the Lord proclaimed the good news to lowly shepherds.

Do you think it strange that this glad word was not first given to the priests, the scholars, or the Pharisees? The reason is clear: God speaks to those who are prepared in their hearts to listen. Apparently these humble shepherds were prepared, and therefore able to discern the voice from Heaven above the noisy din of earth's confusion.

And there were shepherds living out in the fields nearby, keeping watch over their flocks at night.

LUKE 2:8

JANUARY 7

We know we ought to know more about the Bible—but perhaps you're like many Christians: It's so overwhelming you've never really gotten into it.

The first step is to realize what it is: God's "love letter" to you. From one end to the other it tells of God's love for us—a love so great that He sent His Son into the world to redeem us. You wouldn't ignore a letter from someone who loved you; don't ignore God's love letter either.

The unfolding of your words gives light; it gives understanding to the simple.
PSALM 119:130

DECEMBER 23

We hear great cries for tolerance—but consider the bigotry toward Jesus.

There is no room for His Word in our culture, where our children are without reverence for God or faith in the Bible. There is no room for our Lord's creed of purity and self-denial when the media sends forth a constant barrage of profanity and indecency and materialism. There is no room for the promise of His cross and His blood. The angel's statement "He will save his people from their sins" (Matthew 1:21) is rejected by those who deny that the Child in the manger is our Emmanuel, God with us.

There was no room for them in the inn.

LUKE 2:7

JANUARY 8

The Bible tells us that we have two sets of eyes. We have physical eyes—but we also have spiritual "eyes." With one set we see the physical world around us, while with the other we discern the spiritual truths God has set forth for us in His Word.

When we come to Christ, He comes to live within us by His Holy Spirit—and He then opens our spiritual "eyes" to God's truth. This is one reason why the Bible is important, because God uses it to help us discern His truth.

They have eyes to see but do not see and ears to hear but do not hear, for they are a rebellious people.

EZEKIEL 12:2

DECEMBER 22

Jesus was born during the height of the Roman Empire. Unlike previous empires, the Romans built roads from one end of their vast territory to the other. These highways enabled the early Christians to spread the news about Jesus throughout the civilized world in only a few decades—something they never could have done if Jesus had come earlier.

Also, by then the human race had tried all kinds of religions and philosophies, yet none had satisfied the deepest longings of the human heart or taken away the burden of guilt. Many people were now open to His message of hope and new life.

Know that God's timing is always perfect. It was then—and it is today.

When the time had fully come, God sent his Son, born of a woman.
GALATIANS 4:4

JANUARY 9

Never forget: God doesn't want us to just feel His presence.
He wants to change our lives. He wants to take away our
self-centeredness and make us more like Christ. He also wants
to teach us His truth and prepare us to become His servants.

How does this happen? How does God change us into the people
He wants us to be? Not just by a walk in the woods, as pleasant
as that may be. No, God mainly changes us by His Word,
the Bible, as we listen to its truth and allow it to shape our lives.

We...are being transformed into [Christ's] likeness with ever-increasing glory.
2 CORINTHIANS 3:18

DECEMBER 21

This great mystery of God's incarnation—of God coming to earth in the person of Jesus—is the message over which rationalists stumble, humanists are offended, and the world is bewildered. The unbelieving mind is confused by this truth, which runs counter to human wisdom.

Sinful people are incapable of coming to God by their own efforts, so God in love and mercy descended to earth to save us. The creature could not go up to the Creator—so the Creator came down to redeem His creation. May the Holy Spirit of God confirm in your heart the wondrous mystery of the Incarnation.

The Word was God...[and] the Word became
flesh and made his dwelling among us.

JOHN 1:1, 14

JANUARY 10

Why is there so little peace in a world of unprecedented knowledge and unlimited potential? The problem, Jesus said, is the human heart: "out of the heart proceed evil thoughts, murders, adulteries" (Matthew 15:19 NKJV). The new world will come about only when Jesus Christ, the King of kings and the Lord of lords, reigns supreme in people's hearts. At the end of the present age God will act, and Scripture promises that He will act dramatically and decisively. But before that time comes, God wants to rule in our hearts.

I will give you a new heart and put a new spirit in you;
I will remove from you your heart of stone and give you a heart of flesh.
EZEKIEL 36:26

DECEMBER 20

Mary was a virgin, engaged to a godly man by the name of Joseph,
yet she was to be made pregnant supernaturally by the Holy Spirit.
People would talk, shame would be attached to the pregnancy,
and Joseph would probably leave her. But by faith Mary said to Gabriel,
"I am the Lord's servant. May it be to me as you have said" (Luke 1:38).

Mary accepted God's will for her life, no matter what it might cost her.
Following her example, I pray that God would give me grace and courage
to be faithful to Him, no matter what price I may be called on to pay.

*The angel said to her, "Rejoice, highly favored one, the Lord is with you;
blessed are you among women!... And behold, you will conceive in your
womb and bring forth a Son, and shall call His name JESUS."*

LUKE 1:28, 31 NKJV

JANUARY 11

King Solomon was convinced he knew how to find happiness—and because he had vast resources at his command, he was able to pursue it. And yet after gaining everything he had ever wanted, he reluctantly concluded that his life was still empty and without meaning. His search for lasting happiness had failed, and his soul was still empty.

Are you in danger of making the same mistake King Solomon made—convinced that the things of this world will bring you happiness and peace, and pursuing them with all your might? Don't be deceived; they never will. And the reason is because you were made to know God.

I denied myself nothing.... Yet when I surveyed all that my hands had done and what I had toiled to achieve, everything was meaningless.

ECCLESIASTES 2:10–11

DECEMBER 19

The famed movie director Cecil B. DeMille once told me that his film
The King of Kings, made during the silent-movie era, was seen by
an estimated 800 million people. I asked him why he didn't reproduce
The King of Kings with sound and color. He replied, "I will never be
able to do it, because if I gave Jesus a southern accent, the northerners
would not think of Him as their Christ. If I gave Him a foreign accent,
the Americans and the British would not think of Him as their Christ.
As it is, people of all nations, from every race, creed, clan,
can accept Him as their Christ."

*Today in the town of David a Savior has
been born to you; he is Christ the Lord.*

LUKE 2:11

JANUARY 12

When was the last time you truly worshiped God? What is worship anyway?

Worship in the truest sense takes place only when our full attention is on God—on His glory, His power, His majesty, His love, His compassion. And if we're honest, this doesn't happen very often, because even in church or in our times of quiet devotion we get distracted and fail to see God as He truly is.

Learn to shut out the distractions that keep you from truly worshiping God.

Come, let us bow down in worship, let us kneel before the Lord our Maker; for he is our God and we are the people of his pasture, the flock under his care.

PSALM 95:6–7

DECEMBER 18

Jesus Christ lived only thirty-three years, yet He transformed civilization.
And after two thousand years, countless millions worship Him.

Where did He come from? When He was born of the virgin Mary
in a stable in Bethlehem, that was not his origin; that was His
incarnation—His coming in the flesh. The Bible teaches that He is
God in human flesh, God Incarnate. Jesus—the eternal Son of God
—never had a beginning; He will never have an end.
He always was and He always will be.

Praise Him this holy season!

*The Lord Himself will give you a sign: The virgin will be with
child and will give birth to a son, and will call him
Immanuel [which means God with us.]*

ISAIAH 7:14

JANUARY 13

Can an ancient book that was written by many people over
the course of many centuries have anything to say to us today?
Is the Bible's message honestly relevant?

Yes, it is—as millions of believers around the world would attest.
If anything, in fact, it's more relevant today than ever before,
as we see the storm clouds gathering and events taking place that
herald the second coming of Jesus Christ. As the Bible says,
"Our salvation is nearer than when we first believed" (Romans 13:11).

*They asked each other, "Were not our hearts burning within us while he talked with us
on the road and opened the Scriptures to us?"*

LUKE 24:32

DECEMBER 17

Discouragement and depression can come for many reasons.
We all brush up against them—when we lose someone to death,
for example, or experience a problem that overwhelms us.
Depression may even come from chemical imbalances in our bodies;
when that is the case, modern medicine often can help.

At the same time, when we feel discouraged or depressed we need
to turn to God in prayer and commit the situation into His hands.
This isn't a substitute for medical treatment if we need it; God ordained
the physical laws that govern our bodies, and He can use the insights
of medical science to bring healing. But ultimately...when we face
problems of any kind we need to turn to Him.

Be joyful in hope, patient in affliction, faithful in prayer.

ROMANS 12:12

JANUARY 14

How do we put love into action? Serve one another. The Lord modeled this when He washed His disciples' feet. Be patient with one another. This is possible because of the Spirit's presence in us. Be courteous to one another. Even if someone is difficult or disagreeable, treat them with gentleness and love. Set an example for one another "in speech, in life, in love, in faith and in purity" (1 Timothy 4:12).

Edify one another. We are to encourage and build up our brothers and sisters in Christ. Pray for one another. What a privilege to come before the Lord on another's behalf.

Since God so loved us, we also ought to love one another.
No one has ever seen God; but if we love one another,
God lives in us and his love is made complete in us.

1 John 4:11–12

DECEMBER 16

No Psalm is better known or better loved than Psalm 23, which probably owes its origin (at least humanly speaking) to David's boyhood years as a shepherd. But has it become so familiar to us that we have forgotten its riches?

Look at the verses. They tell us first of all that God is like a shepherd to us—guiding us, keeping us safe, protecting us from our enemies, giving us everything we need to sustain our lives. But they also hint at our tendency to wander and get in trouble, like the lost sheep in one of Jesus' parables (see Luke 15:17).

The Lord is my shepherd, I shall not be in want.
He makes me lie down in green pastures, he leads me
beside quiet waters, he restores my soul.

PSALM 23:1–3

JANUARY 15

Philosophers argued with Paul—but some who heard him were serious searchers after truth. The religions and philosophies of the day had left them empty, and they wanted to know the truth. And they heard it as they listened to Paul tell them about Jesus, and the hope we can have because of Him.

Are you searching for the truth? Don't let anything—or anyone—keep you from Jesus, who alone is "the way and the truth and the life" (John 14:6).

While Paul was… in Athens… he reasoned in the synagogue with the Jews and the God-fearing Greeks, as well as in the marketplace day by day with those who happened to be there.

ACTS 17:16–17

DECEMBER 15

My dictionary defines *wonderful* as anything that is so unusual
or magnificent that it causes wonder and amazement.

Jesus was wonderful in His life. He mingled with sinners,
yet His enemies could find not one single flaw in His character.
His miracles and His teaching both testified to His divine authority.

Christ was also wonderful in His death. He died for others just
as He had lived for others: To make our salvation possible.
And this death led to the wonderful, glorious Resurrection,
opening for us the door to Heaven and eternal life.

Jesus is wonderful indeed!

He will be called Wonderful Counselor, Mighty God,
Everlasting Father, Prince of Peace.

ISAIAH 9:6

JANUARY 16

Suppose a friend comes by your house and offers you a gift. What would you do? Would you refuse to take it until you had paid him for it? Would you decline it because you felt you weren't worthy of it? No, of course not. Your friend wants you to have it and has already paid for it; all you must do is accept it.

In a far greater way, this is what Jesus Christ did for you. By His death on the cross he paid the price for your salvation—completely and fully. Now He offers it to you as a free gift—and all you have to do is receive it.

Ask and it will be given to you; seek and you will find;
knk and the door will be opened to you."

LUKE 11:9

DECEMBER 14

If you took a poll of people you and I pass every day on the street, many would say that the main reason they aren't attracted to the Christian faith—is the Christians they know. Some repel them by their self-righteousness; others show no love or compassion; still others show little concern for the world and its problems. Most of all, they'll point out, Christians can't seem to get along with each other. Why should we believe in Christ (they say) when He doesn't seem to make any difference in the lives of His followers?

Do others see Him in you?

Finally, all of you, live in harmony with one another;
be sympathetic, love as brothers, be compassionate and humble
...because to this you were called.

1 PETER 3:8–9

JANUARY 17

God doesn't necessarily remove all our problems when we become followers of Christ. But He has promised to be with us and help us and encourage us in the midst of those problems.

He loves us and is with us, and nothing we will ever face takes Him by surprise. This peace is also possible because the Holy Spirit gives us patience and joy even in the midst of life's difficulties. And peace is possible because we know our problems are only temporary; someday they will all come to an end.

Present your requests to God. And the peace of God, which transcends all understanding, will guard your hearts and your minds in Christ Jesus.

PHILIPPIANS 4:6–7

DECEMBER 13

Does God honestly care about what is going on in our lives? When hard times hit or illness strikes, does He really care?

The answer is "Yes—a thousand times yes!" When the apostle Paul wrote these words he had just endured one of the hardest times in his life: "We were under great pressure, far beyond our ability to endure, so that we despaired even of life" (2 Corinthians 1:8). But in the midst of it God assured him of His compassion and presence, and in time God brought Paul through the trials he was experiencing and opened the door to new opportunities.

Praise be to the God and Father of our Lord Jesus Christ, the Father of compassion and the God of all comfort, who comforts us in all our troubles, so that we can comfort those in any trouble.

2 CORINTHIANS 1:3–4

JANUARY 18

Do you feel as if you've let God down? Let me reassure you that He loves you no matter what you've done. The last thing God wants you to do is to spend your life filled with guilt and shame and remorse.

May that truth give you hope, because it means that God wants to help you. He wants to put back together the pieces of your life and make you whole.

So if you feel as if you've failed God, ask for His forgiveness— and ask Him also to help you forgive yourself for what you have done. Then commit your future to Him.

Though I walk in the midst of trouble, you preserve my life.

PSALM 138:7

DECEMBER 12

Can you blame Abraham and Sarah for doubting God's promise that within a year she would bear a son? Sarah had been childless all their married life, and now she was approaching the age of ninety. [But] the impossible happened: Isaac was born.

Remember Abraham and Sarah the next time you encounter what seems to be an insurmountable problem. Nothing was too hard for God then—and nothing is too hard for Him today. If it were, why would we pray? But God is still sovereign over His creation, and He is still at work. That doesn't mean He always answers the way we wish He would—but never doubt His power, and never doubt His love.

Is anything too hard for the Lord? I will return to you at the appointed time next year and Sarah will have a son.

GENESIS 18:14

JANUARY 19

The most important advice for life's crossroads is this:
"Seek God's will." He knows what's best for you, and He doesn't
want you to wander aimlessly through life.

Never forget: God made you, and He knows all about you—including
the gifts and abilities He gave you. More than that, He loves you and
wants what is best for you. Maybe you've been living for yourself and
for the moment rather than for Him and for things eternal.
But don't stay on that path; you will only end up at a blank wall
if you ignore God's plan for your life.

I will instruct you and teach you in the way you should go;
I will counsel you and watch over you.

PSALM 32:8

DECEMBER 11

[Christmas is] such a busy time, and our spending easily gets out of control. Instead of a season of peace and goodwill, it becomes a season of exhaustion and resentment. Of course Christmas shouldn't be this way—nor does it need to be.

There is a deeper solution to having a good Christmas—and that is to rediscover its true meaning. At Christmas we celebrate the birth of Jesus Christ, who came down from Heaven to save us from our sins. May you see His glory this Christmas season!

When they saw the star, they were overjoyed. On coming to the house, they saw the child with his mother Mary, and they bowed down and worshiped.

MATTHEW 2:10–11

JANUARY 20

Artists throughout the centuries have tried to imagine what [Jesus] must have looked like, but the truth is, we don't know.

Some day we will know what the risen Christ looks like, for someday we will enter into His presence forever. And when we do, the Bible says, "we shall be like him, for we shall see him as he is" (1 John 3:2). Then we will share in His resurrection glory, and we will share in His sinless perfection.

He had no beauty or majesty to attract us to him,
nothing in his appearance that we should desire him.

ISAIAH 53:2

DECEMBER 10

Jesus [said] that nothing—absolutely nothing
—must stand in the way of being His disciple.

Many people are willing to have Jesus as part of their lives
—as long as it doesn't cost them anything. They may even
profess faith in Jesus and join a church. But Jesus to them is almost like
an insurance policy—something they obtain and then forget about
until they die. But Jesus calls us to follow Him every day.
What keeps you from being His disciple?

Another disciple said to him, "Lord, first let me go and bury my father."
But Jesus told him, "Follow me, and let the dead bury their own dead!"

MATTHEW 8:21–22

JANUARY 21

People often have one of three reactions to the message of the Gospel.
First, some people will deny the Gospel is true. They laugh and scoff.
Pride may prompt this scorn. Others fear what people would think,
so they don't give credence to God's truth.

Second, some people delay. They say, "I'll think about it
and maybe make a commitment to follow Jesus some other time."
But it's dangerous to delay making a decision, because you
may never hear the gospel again.

Third, some people will make a decision for Christ, even though they
know that being a believer may place them in a minority.

If the world hates you, keep in mind that it hated me first.

JOHN 15:18

DECEMBER 9

On that memorable night in the Judean hills of Bethlehem two thousand years ago, this was the song of the angels. Though the centuries have rolled by, still the world longs for and looks for the peace that the angels announced. Where is this peace?

Clearly it is not evident in the world, with its constant fighting and conflicts. This peace abides instead in the hearts of all those who have trusted in God's grace. In the same proportion that the world has trusted Christ, it has peace. There can be no lasting peace until Christ has come to the hearts of all people and brought them His peace.

Glory to God in the highest, and on earth peace
to men on whom his favor rests."

LUKE 2:14

JANUARY 22

Eating right, exercising regularly, and sleeping adequately—
these are some of the components of a physically healthy life.
And God wants us to take care of the body He has given us.
The Bible says, "your body is a temple of the Holy Spirit...
Therefore honor God with your body" (1 Corinthians 6:19–20).

But we can give too much attention to our bodies and almost worship them
by giving them the amount of attention that only God deserves. We can
focus on our physical health so much that we ignore the health of our soul.

*For physical training is of some value, but godliness has value
for all things, holding promise for both the present life and the life to come.*

TIMOTHY 4:8

DECEMBER 8

It's true; life is short, and the older you get the more you realize it. Events that happened thirty years ago seem like they took place just yesterday—but when your mind turns to the future, you realize just how short life is. None of us knows how much more time we'll have, but even if God gives us a long life by most standards, our time is still brief. In the Psalmist's words, "Each man's life is but a breath" (Psalm 39:5).

Don't waste your life on things that have no eternal value. Draw closer to Christ, and make each day count for Him.

Show me, O Lord, my life's end and the number of my days; let me know how fleeting my life is."

PSALM 39:4

JANUARY 23

Problems and struggles can wear us down physically, emotionally, and mentally—and can even erode our faith.

But God, our loving heavenly Father, understands our feelings at times like these, and He wants to encourage and help us. After all, His Son, Jesus Christ, went through the same experiences we do—although without sinning (see Hebrews 4:15). We are never alone when we know Christ, and we can trust Him to lead us and point the way out of our dilemma.

Life sometimes takes us through hard places. But even in the midst of them, God is with us, and nothing can happen to us that is beyond His ability to help.

As a father has compassion on his children, so the Lord has compassion on those who fear him; for he knows how we are formed.

PSALM 103:13–14

DECEMBER 7

How do you draw the line between your own desires and
God's will for you? It isn't always easy.

The question of our motives—why we do what we do—is always with us.
It's not wrong to enjoy something, as long as it's good and honorable.
God may even have gifted you in certain ways, and it would be wrong to
deny those gifts. But always commit your motives to Christ and seek His
will in everything—even in things you enjoy.

*Delight yourself in the Lord and he will
give you the desires of your heart.*

PSALM 37:4

JANUARY 24

Little did the disciples know what Jesus would do with only five loaves and two fish. The Bible tells us that everyone in the crowd ate—and there were twelve basketfuls of leftovers.

Perhaps when you give to your church or some other ministry, your thinking is like that of the disciples: "I can only give...." Give what you can give—and give in faith.

After all, Jesus only had a few loaves of bread and a couple of fish, but in His hands God multiplied it, and it became a huge feast for the crowd.

We have only five loaves of bread and two fish.
LUKE 9:13

DECEMBER 6

When we keep on sinning without ever attempting to turn from it or restrain it, it is because we are still sin's slaves.

Never forget that sin is God's enemy—and Satan's friend. Sin is so serious that it caused Jesus Christ to leave Heaven's glory and come into the world to die as the final and complete sacrifice for sin. Don't take sin lightly. Repent of it when it rears its ugly head, and with God's help cast it out of your life.

What shall we say then? Shall we go on sinning so that grace may increase? By no means! We died to sin; how can we live in it any longer?

ROMANS 6:1–2

JANUARY 25

It's significant that after the giving of the commandments is the story of the building of the sacrificial altar. The Ten Commandments were given first, but the law and the altar go together. The law reveals that we are sinners and that we need forgiveness. But the law also reveals that the only path to forgiveness is through sacrifice. The law enables us to see ourselves as morally dirty and in need of cleansing. But it also points us to the place of cleansing: the cross of Christ.

No one will be declared righteous in [God's] sight by observing the law; rather, through the law we become conscious of sin.

ROMANS 3:20

DECEMBER 5

The person who is in the most danger spiritually is the one who doesn't see any need for God. They may enjoy life; they may be successful and looked up to by others. They may moral and honest, and even be outwardly religious (although only outwardly, because it hasn't touched their hearts).

Do you know people like this—even in your own family? Only God can break through the barrier of a heart that has no place for Him. That is why the most important thing you can do is to pray for them. Don't give up; God is able to do what we cannot do.

In them is fulfilled the prophecy of Isaiah: "You will be ever hearing but never understanding; you will be ever seeing but never perceiving."

MATTHEW 13:14

JANUARY 26

When you were very young and first started speaking, did you talk to your parents in long sentences and for great lengths of time? I doubt it. And yet they weren't disappointed in you; they were delighted by your first attempts to speak.

In the same way, when we truly understand that God is our loving heavenly Father and we are His children, then we won't worry so much about disappointing Him by our prayers. Don't worry about your lack of eloquence; no matter how simple they are, God delights in our prayers when they truly express the feelings and desires of our heart.

Oh that men would praise the Lord for his goodness,
and for his wonderful works to the children of men!
PSALM 107:8 KJV

DECEMBER 4

Repeatedly Jesus made the most startling claim imaginable:
He was God in human flesh. He wasn't just a man (although He was that);
He was also God. Think of it: The great and powerful God of the universe
came down to earth and took upon Himself human flesh!

But His teaching about Himself didn't stop there. He went on to
say that because He was divine, He was without sin—and because He
was without sin, He could become the sin-bearer for the human race.
All our sins would be placed on Him, and He would take upon Himself
the death and Hell we deserve.

Anyone who has seen me has seen the Father.

JOHN 14:9

JANUARY 27

God knows everything about us, even our deepest thoughts and motives. We can hide them from other people; we may even hide them from ourselves. But we can't hide them from God.

This shouldn't surprise us; after all, God knows everything. The Bible says, "Nothing in all creation is hidden from God's sight. Everything is uncovered and laid bare before the eyes of him to whom we must give account" (Hebrews 4:13). Think back over just the last twenty-four hours at all the thoughts you didn't want anyone else to know. But God knew them—every one of them.

You alone know the hearts of all men.

1 KINGS 8:39

DECEMBER 3

When God opens a door, what possible excuse can we
have for not going through it?

All over the world God is opening doors of opportunity today,
making it possible for us to take the Gospel to millions who have
never heard of Christ. Some live in lands that have been freed in recent
years from the grip of atheism; others are immersed in a rising tide
of secularism or religious oppression. But in spite of the barriers
—and they are real—God is opening doors today in unexpected ways
for the preaching of the Gospel. Will we fail to go through them?

*What he opens no one can shut, and what he shuts no one can open
.... See, I have placed before you an open door that no one can shut.*

REVELATION 3:7–8

JANUARY 28

Have you ever noticed that if you continue to hate someone, whatever they did will continue to hurt you? Our anger and hatred just keeps reopening the emotional wounds of the past.

This is one reason why we need to let go of the past and—with God's help—release our anger and hatred and replace them with His love. If we don't our souls will be poisoned the rest of our life by bitterness and resentment, instead of reflecting the love and mercy of Christ. Remember Jesus' command: "Love your enemies and pray for those who persecute you" (Matthew 5:44).

Get rid of all bitterness, rage and anger, brawling and slander, along with every form of malice.

EPHESIANS 4:31

DECEMBER 2

It's natural to wonder what Heaven must be like. Are the streets really paved with gold? Will we know each other? What will we do with our time? These and a hundred other questions crowd our minds—and to be honest, the Bible doesn't answer all our questions about Heaven.

But one truth about Heaven is absolutely clear: We will be safely in God's presence forever. All the fears and insecurities and sorrows and disappointments that afflict us here will be banished. So too will all the weaknesses and sins and failures that mark our lives right now. We will be changed—for we will be like Christ!

We know that when he appears, we shall be like him,
for we shall see him as he is.

1 JOHN 3:2

JANUARY 29

What spiritual gifts has God given you? They won't be the same as someone else's gifts—but they are the ones God knew you needed.

Don't say your gifts are insignificant or don't matter; God didn't make a mistake when He gave them to you.

You may have a special gift for welcoming visitors to your church, or helping the church's nursery, or praying for others, or becoming part of a team that does errands for sick people. It may be helping in a homeless shelter or packing boxes of clothing to ship overseas.

*We have different gifts.... If it is serving, let him serve;
if it is teaching, let him teach; if it is encouraging,
let him encourage...if it is showing mercy, let him do it cheerfully.*

ROMANS 12:6–8

DECEMBER 1

Recently I heard about the owner of a small factory who was greatly respected by his employees—not only for his business skills, but for his integrity and his concern for his employees. They knew he went out of his way to be fair to them, and that more than once during hard times he sacrificed the company's profits to keep his workers employed.

After his death one of his long-time employees was showing the man's grandson around the factory.

"This was the secret of his success," he said. "Every morning he slipped in here before anyone else arrived, and spent at least half an hour in prayer."

But when you pray, go into your room, close the door and pray to your Father, who is unseen. Then your Father, who sees what is done in secret, will reward you.

MATTHEW 6:6

JANUARY 30

When life turns against us and we can't see any way out of our problems, is He still with us—even if it looks as if He has abandoned us? Can His promises really be trusted?

Yes, we can trust His promises—because God does not lie, nor does He change His mind. What if He did? Then we wouldn't have any reason to depend on Him; His Word could not be trusted. But He doesn't lie, and He doesn't change His mind—because He is perfect and holy, and He loves us.

*God is not a man, that he should lie, nor a son of man,
that he should change his mind.*

NUMBERS 23:19

NOVEMBER 30

Jesus welcomed the children who flocked around Him:
"Let the little children come to me, and do not hinder them,
for the kingdom of heaven belongs to such as these" (Matthew 19:14).
Their openness, their enthusiasm, their trust—all these delighted Jesus.
A young child may not understand everything about God—but he or
she can understand something. A young child understands love,
and also understands what it means to obey someone. Don't ignore
the children God brings across your path, but by your words and by
your example tell them about Jesus.

He called a little child and had him stand among them....
And he said..." whoever humbles himself like this little child is
the greatest in the kingdom of heaven."

MATTHEW 18:2–4

JANUARY 31

How much of your time is used for things that really aren't important, or may even be morally or spiritually harmful? Take television or the Internet, for example. We all need to relax, and I'm not suggesting all entertainment is harmful or bad—not at all. But how much of your spare time is simply wasted?

How much time did you give to God? Remember: Satan doesn't need for us to fall into gross sin in order to defeat us; a large dose of laziness will do the trick just as well. Put Christ first in your life, and then commit every hour of the day to Him.

Be diligent in these matters; give yourself wholly to them, so that everyone may see your progress.
1 TIMOTHY 4:15

NOVEMBER 29

Many of us—and society as a whole—have tried to bypass God, and now we are paying the inevitable price. We are in trouble because we have left out God; we have left out the Ten Commandments; we have left out the Sermon on the Mount. Now we as individuals and as a culture are reaping the tragic results.

But the living Christ can bring glorious hope to us and to our world. After His Resurrection, Jesus promised, "I am with you always."

Surely I am with you always, to the very end of the age.
MATTHEW 28:20

FEBRUARY 1

Thankfully slavery is a thing of the past for us—but the underlying principle the apostle Paul gives us here still stands: If we are employers or supervisors, we are to do "what is right and fair" to those who work under us. After all, he reminds us, we, too, have a Master, and someday we'll give an account of our lives to Him—including how we treat others.

This principle holds for all of us—for it is just another way of expressing Jesus' words to His disciples: "In everything, do to others what you would have them do to you" (Matthew 7:12). Write this principle on your heart—and put it into action every day.

*Masters, provide your slaves with what is right and fair,
because you know that you also have a Master in heaven.*

COLOSSIANS 4:1

NOVEMBER 28

God delights in giving—even to His enemies. He gives people food—but they give Him rebellion. God gives people wisdom —but they serve the devil with it. He gives them strength —but they waste it in evil pursuits.

All of God's giving, however, should drive us to thanksgiving. Whatever material things we enjoy came from God, and He gives them to us to remind us of His goodness.

No matter what we receive from Him, it should drive us to give humble thanks to God, from whom all blessings flow.

He has shown kindness by giving you rain from heaven and crops in their seasons; he provides you with plenty of food and fills your hearts with joy.

ACTS 14:17

FEBRUARY 2

Imagine what the world would be like if God were
only a God of love, who never judged evil or tried to stop it.
Evil men could carry out their plans without fear. They would never
have to worry that God would judge them or try to stop them.

Now imagine what the world would be like if God were
only a God of judgment, who punished us every time we did wrong.
If God were like that, none of us would ever have a chance,
for we sin every day. Sometimes, however, God does correct and
discipline us—not because He hates us, but because He loves us and
wants us to turn from the destructive path we are on.

The Lord is gracious and compassionate, slow to anger.

PSALM 145:8

NOVEMBER 27

Whenever we sit down for a meal, let us not forget that at least half the world goes to bed hungry. When we enjoy the comfort of our home, let us not forget that millions have no home to go to. As we ride in our car, let us not forget that many people in the world cannot afford even a bicycle.

Whenever we go to church to thank God for our material and spiritual blessings, let us remember that millions have never heard the gospel, the good news of salvation in Christ.

May our gratitude find expression in our prayers and our service for others, and in our commitment to live wholly for Christ.

If anyone has material possessions and sees his brother in need but has no pity on him, how can the love of God be in him?

1 JOHN 3:17

FEBRUARY 3

If someone deliberately commits a crime and is caught,
who is to blame if that person is found guilty and sentenced to jail?
Is the judge to blame—or is the criminal?

The lawbreaker is to blame for what has happened to him, not the judge.
Yes, the judge sentenced him, but he alone broke the law, and he alone
is to blame for the penalty he received. The judge was only following the
law. The lawbreaker can't blame the judge; he can only blame himself.

Likewise, when we break God's law, we stand condemned,
and we ourselves are to blame for what happens to us, not God.

*For God did not send his Son into the world to condemn the world,
but to save the world through him.*

JOHN 3:17

NOVEMBER 26

Throughout the Bible we are commanded to be thankful.
A spirit of thanksgiving is one of the most distinctive marks of a
Christian whose heart is attuned to the Lord.

We are to be thankful for the material blessings God gives us.
We need to give thanks for our spouse, our children, our relatives,
and our friends. Most of all, thank God for Christ and His love for you.

Thank God in the midst of trials and ever persecution.
For the Christian, every day is Thanksgiving Day!

Enter [God's] gates with thanksgiving and his courts with praise;
give thanks to him and praise his name.

PSALM 100:4

FEBRUARY 4

If we looked only at the headlines every day, we would have good reason to be pessimistic about the future. But don't forget two important truths.

First, the future is in God's hands, and nothing takes Him by surprise. He is sovereign over the history of the world as well as our own personal histories, and behind the scenes He is at work to accomplish His purposes.

Second, never forget that even when the future is unclear, God is with those of us who are trusting Christ as our Savior and Lord, and He helps us. No matter what the future holds for you—no matter what today holds for you—you do not face it alone if you know Christ.

The Lord reigns forever.
PSALM 146:10

NOVEMBER 25

The Apostle Paul warned that the time would come when "people will be lovers of themselves…ungrateful" (2 Timothy 3:2). What a description of our own times! Rather than being grateful, we get wrapped up in ourselves and take for granted what others do for us. Of course, it shouldn't be this way, but it often is.

I find myself thinking about how ungrateful we often are to God. He has given us everything we have—but are we truly thankful? Most of all, God sent Jesus into the world to die for us. Have we responded by thanking Him for His love, and giving our life to Him?

Thanks be to God for his indescribable gift!
2 CORINTHIANS 9:15

FEBRUARY 5

The opening chapters of the Bible tell us that the Garden of Eden was perfect—a place given by God to Adam and Eve so that their every need would be met. The reason the garden was perfect was because sin had not yet entered the world. But when Adam and Eve listened to Satan and turned against God—when Adam and Eve sinned—that perfect garden was no longer perfect. God banished them from the garden, and they would never return.

But that is not the end of the story. Christ came to conquer sin and death—and He has! In Him there is hope!

Now the Lord God had planted a garden in the east, in Eden; and there he put the man he had formed.

GENESIS 2:8

NOVEMBER 24

The Pilgrim Fathers who landed at Plymouth to settle in what became the United States of America can teach us an important lesson about giving thanks.

During that first long winter, seven times as many graves were made for the dead as homes were made for the living. Seed, imported from England, failed to grow, and a ship that was to bring food and relief, brought instead thirty-five more mouths to feed, but no provisions.

According to today's standards, the Pilgrims had almost nothing, but they possessed a profound and heartfelt gratitude to God for His love and mercy. Gratitude is one of the greatest Christian virtues.

Now, our God, we give you thanks, And praise your glorious name.

1 CHRONICLES 29:13

FEBRUARY 6

Queen Victoria...would sometimes go into the slums of London. One day she went into a home to have tea with an older woman. When she rose to leave, the queen asked, "Is there anything I can do for you?"

The woman said, "Yes, Your Majesty. You can meet me in Heaven." The queen turned to her and said softly, "Yes. I'll be there, but only because of the blood that was shed on the cross for you and for me." Queen Victoria, in her day the most powerful woman in the world, had to depend on the blood of Christ for her salvation. And so do we.

At the name of Jesus every knee should bow, in heaven and on earth and under the earth, and every tongue confess that Jesus Christ is Lord, to the glory of God the Father.

PHILIPPIANS 2:10–11

NOVEMBER 23

Separated from friends, unjustly accused, brutally treated
—if any man had a right to complain, it was this man, languishing
almost forgotten in a harsh Roman prison. But instead of complaints,
his lips rang with words of praise and thanksgiving!

This was the apostle Paul, a man who had learned to give thanks
even in the midst of great adversity. Look carefully at what he wrote
during his prison experience: "Sing and make music in your heart to
the Lord, always giving thanks to God the Father for everything,
in the name of our Lord Jesus Christ" (Ephesians 5:19–20).

I have learned the secret of being content in any and every situation,
whether well fed or hungry, whether living in plenty or in want.

PHILIPPIANS 4:12

FEBRUARY 7

Satan does not build a church and call it the First Church of Satan —he is far too clever for that. Instead, he tries to infiltrate the theological seminary and the pulpit, invading the church under the cover of an orthodox vocabulary—but emptying sacred terms of their true biblical meaning or denying their truth.

The sword of the Spirit—the Bible—is the weapon God has provided for us to use in this battle between truth and deception. Make it a priority to wield that sword skillfully. God's followers need to know the truth He sets forth in His Word so that we can confidently discern between His truth and Satan's lies.

Watch out for false prophets. They come to you in sheep's clothing, but inwardly they are ferocious wolves.

MATTHEW 7:15

NOVEMBER 22

Ingratitude and thanklessness are far too common in our world. Children forget to thank their parents for all they do. Common courtesy is scorned. People take for granted the way others help them. And, above all, we fail to thank God for His blessings. Such an ungrateful heart is cold toward God and indifferent to His mercy and love. It is a heart that has forgotten how dependent we are on God for everything.

Be like that one leper: Take time to give thanks—and mean it.

Give thanks to the Lord, for he is good; his love endures forever.

PSALM 107:1

FEBRUARY 8

Children are not shy about asking for things. They would not be normal if they didn't boldly make their desires known. God is keenly aware that we are dependent on Him for life's necessities, so we can freely ask Him for those things. God loves us, and He knows our needs and wants to grant them to us. The Bible says, "No good thing will He withhold from those who walk uprightly" (Psalm 84:11 NKJV).

How great is the love the Father has lavished on us,
that we should be called children of God! And that is what we are!

1 JOHN 3:1

NOVEMBER 21

How does God define success? His measure is very different from the world's measure, and it can be summed up in one sentence: Success in God's eyes is faithfulness to His calling. Paul was a failure in the world's eyes—but not to God. Even Jesus was a failure as far as most people were concerned, but "he was faithful to the one who appointed him"—and that is all that mattered.

What is your definition of success? Is it the same as God's —and are you pursuing it?

Therefore, holy brothers, who share in the heavenly calling, fix your thoughts on Jesus.... He was faithful to the one who appointed him.

HEBREWS 3:1–2

FEBRUARY 9

The heart is the seat of our emotions, the seat of decisive action, and the seat of belief (as well as doubt). The heart symbolizes the center of our moral, spiritual, and intellectual life. It is the seat of our conscience and life.

And God knows our heart well. The Almighty God searches our heart, weighs our heart by the teaching of Scripture, opens our heart to His truth, and gives us a new heart when we come to Christ—a heart of flesh sensitive to His presence, His leading, and His love. Don't ever hesitate to take to Him whatever is on your heart. He already knows it anyway, but He doesn't want you to bear its pain or celebrate its joy alone.

Man looks at the outward appearance, but the Lord looks at the heart.
1 SAMUEL 16:7

NOVEMBER 20

Jesus Christ isn't just the center of the Bible; He is the center of our lives. By believing in Him, John says, we "have life in his name." What does this mean? First, it means eternal life. Without Christ we have no hope of Heaven; as the Bible says, "the wages of sin is death" (Romans 6:23). But when we yield our lives to Christ and trust Him alone for our salvation, we know we will be with Him through all eternity.

But Jesus Christ also gives us life right now—not the artificial, unstable life the world offers, but a life of purpose and peace and joy. Is Christ the center of your life?

But these are written that you may believe that Jesus is the Christ, the Son of God, and that by believing you may have life in his name.

JOHN 20:31

FEBRUARY 10

In a sense, you and I get programmed. When we are young, our minds are constantly being programmed by the experiences we have. This programming happens to all of us. But when the things that have been put into our memories are bad or untrue, we will have problems later in life.

In that case, we need to reprogram our mind and heart; we need to replace the bad things that have taken root there with good and true things. And that is where God can help. In His Word, He provides truths to replace the lies you've believed about yourself.

You are precious and honored in my sight, and...I love you.

ISAIAH 43:4

NOVEMBER 19

Without Barzillai the history of God's people might have been vastly different. In one of the saddest events in the Bible, King David's son Absalom revolted against his father and attempted to take the throne by force. David and his men had to flee for their lives, and by the time they reached the vicinity of Barzillai's home they were out of supplies and in danger of starvation. But Barzillai came to their aid and David's army was saved.

Barzillai was eighty when this happened, and he easily could have said, "I'm too old to do anything," or "It's too risky; what if Absalom wins?" But he didn't.

Now Barzillai was a very old man, eighty years of age. He had provided for the king during his stay in Mahanaim.

2 SAMUEL 19:32

FEBRUARY 11

Too many people think God is to be found by looking within our own minds and souls, and they often cite these words of Jesus in support of their claim.

Jesus, however, wasn't teaching that God is within us, and that all we need to do is look inward to find God. Instead, Jesus was talking to people who believed that the Messiah would establish an earthly, political kingdom—and Jesus said that wasn't His goal. "My kingdom is not of this world," Jesus told Pilate (John 18:36). His goal instead was to rule in the hearts of men and women.

The kingdom of God is within you.
Luke 17:20

NOVEMBER 18

Is faith illogical, as some would have you believe? No, not at all.
Some of the most brilliant people I have ever known were also men
and women of deep faith in Christ, and without exception they said they
believed in the Gospel because it made sense. Believing our intricate world
happened by accident, they said, takes more faith than believing in God!

But there was another reason for their faith: They were convinced
Jesus Christ was who He claimed to be: God in human flesh,
sent to save us from our sins.

*For since the creation of the world God's invisible qualities
—his eternal power and divine nature—have been clearly seen,
being understood from what has been made.*

ROMANS 1:20

FEBRUARY 12

As was the custom of the day, the man afflicted with leprosy had called out "Unclean! Unclean!" to warn people of his presence so they could avoid him. Who knows how long it had been since he had experienced a human touch—a warm embrace, an encouraging pat on the back, a friendly handshake? Had it been months, or even years?

Jesus knew the man needed relief from this disease, but before Jesus dealt with his skin, He healed the man's emotional pain. Jesus reached out and touched him. Can you imagine how that leper felt when someone actually touched him? Then Jesus freed him from his leprosy.

Filled with compassion, Jesus reached out his hand and touched the man.

MARK 1:41

NOVEMBER 17

Once we come to Christ we are no longer just individuals.
We are now members of His family—what the Bible here calls
"the church, his body". We are now part of that vast group of people
throughout the ages who have trusted Christ and are our brothers and
sisters in His family. Although we'll never meet most of them this side of
eternity, we're still united spiritually with them. This transcends any local
church or denomination; it includes all who truly belong to Christ.

Christ is the head of the church, his body, of which he is the Savior.
EPHESIANS 5:23

FEBRUARY 13

Too often people are filled with regret and guilt because they failed to reach out to someone with whom they were at odds—and then death intervenes and it's too late. Don't let this happen to you. If a broken relationship comes to mind, know that the place to begin is within yourself. Are you convinced that rebuilding this relationship is something God wants you to do?

Then let the person know that you care, and that you want your relationship to be different. Don't use words alone; back up your words with action.

Make every effort to live in peace with all men and to be holy.

HEBREWS 12:14

NOVEMBER 16

Being a parent is hard; every child is different,
and every day brings fresh challenges.

First, see your children as a gift from God. He entrusted them to you;
take them as a gift (and responsibility) from His hands. Second, let them
know you love them. Show affection for them; teach them right and
wrong; spend time with them. Third, be an example of faith. Pray with
them, read the Bible to them, and let them see that Christ is important
to you. With God's help, you can be the kind of parent they need.

*Train a child in the way he should go,
and when he is old he will not turn from it.*

PROVERBS 22:6

FEBRUARY 14

Prejudice or hatred of any person because of their racial, ethnic, or religious background is wrong. God labels it sin.

After all, God created every one of us, and when we hate someone who is different from us, we are hating someone whom God has made and who is valuable in His sight. Every human being is created in God's image, and although sin has blurred that image in all of us, every single one of us still bears the mark of our Creator. Jesus didn't die to save just one race or one group of people; Jesus died for all.

Let no debt remain outstanding, except the continuing debt to love one another, for he who loves his fellowman has fulfilled the law.

ROMANS 13:8

NOVEMBER 15

Life is hard, and our years on earth are marked by "trouble and sorrow."
As someone has said, there is no false advertising in the Bible!

We wish it weren't so, of course; maybe that's why we're
so quick to believe the advertisements that promise
happiness if we'll only use their product.

We live in a world that is broken because of sin,
and we share in its brokenness.

What difference should this make? First, it should give us greater
compassion for others. Second, it should make us yearn for Heaven.

The length of our days is seventy years...yet their span is but trouble and sorrow.

PSALM 90:10

FEBRUARY 15

The command to forgive as we have been forgiven is difficult to obey, but we need to forgive people who have wronged us—even if we don't think they deserve it. If we don't, the poisons of anger and bitterness will eat away at our souls—but with God's help we can deal with them in a way that honors Him.

If we were at fault in any way, we need to face it honestly and seek God's forgiveness. Then we need to ask the person to forgive us as well—even if they may refuse.

Bear with each other and forgive whatever grievances you may have against one another. Forgive as the Lord forgave you.

COLOSSIANS 3:13

NOVEMBER 14

We all experience discouragement,
and sometimes it can be almost overwhelming.

Elijah...had been one of God's most faithful servants,
never wavering in the face of disaster. God used Elijah to overcome
the pagan prophets of Baal and demonstrate to all the nation that
God alone was worthy of their worship.

But now, only days later, discouragement and depression have almost
overwhelmed him. ...Elijah flees into the desert and concludes he is a failure.

God showed Him His glory, reminding Elijah of the greatness
of the God he served. When discouragement comes and you wonder
if you can go on, remember Elijah—and be encouraged.

*[Elijah] came to a broom tree, sat down under it and prayed that he
might die. "I have had enough, Lord," he said.*

1 KINGS 19:4

FEBRUARY 16

Have you ever asked yourself why it's so hard to apologize?
One reason is pride: We hate to admit we were wrong. But the Bible
says that pride is sin: "I hate pride and arrogance" (Proverbs 8:13).

So if apologizing is difficult for you, ask God to help you
overcome your pride—or whatever else is holding you back.
Seek out one person you may have hurt and say very simply,
"I'm sorry." Next time, apologizing will be even easier.

Be completely humble and gentle.
EPHESIANS 4:2

NOVEMBER 13

Jesus was warning His disciples that it would be costly for them to follow Him. It would be costly because they would have to give up their own plans and goals...because they must share in His rejection and death. No wonder "many of his disciples turned back and no longer followed him" (John 6:66).

The cost of following Jesus has not changed. We want to cling to our plans—but He says they must go. We want to live for ourselves —but He says we must live for Him. We want to live a life of pleasure and ease—but He says we must follow Him to the cross.

If anyone would come after me, he must deny himself and take up his cross daily and follow me.

LUKE 9:23

FEBRUARY 17

Imagine for a minute that you committed a crime,
were arrested, and put in jail.

As you stand before the judge, there is absolutely no doubt:
you are guilty of the charges against you. According to the law,
you must pay for this crime, and in this case the penalty is a year in jail.
The judge issues his verdict and pronounces your sentence.

But then something almost beyond belief happens. The judge steps
down from the bench, stops the bailiff, and takes your place.
He is innocent—but he goes to prison and pays the penalty for the
crime you committed. You, on the other hand, are free!

You have been set free from sin.

ROMANS 6:22

NOVEMBER 12

One of the signs of the latter days before Christ returns, the Bible says, is that "People will be...disobedient to their parents" (2 Timothy 3:2). Instead of obeying the commandment to "Honor your father and your mother," they'll bring dishonor to them.

Does this command become irrelevant as we grow older? Is it only meant for young children? No, not at all. As long as our parents are alive, we are to honor and respect them. They weren't perfect—but they were the ones God gave you, and you should honor them because of that.

Honor your father and your mother,
as the Lord your God has commanded you.

DEUTERONOMY 5:16

FEBRUARY 18

You've heard the expression "Forgive and forget"
—but is it really possible? Perhaps someone once hurt you
very deeply—and the emotional scars still ache in your memory.
The last thing you think you could ever do is forgive and forget.

And yet Jesus goes even farther: He not only tells us to forgive and forget,
but to love the one who hurt us and pray for their welfare. We aren't to
erase them from our memories; we are to keep them in our prayers!

Impossible? Yes—apart from God's help.

You have heard that it was said, "Love your neighbor and hate your enemy."
But I tell you: Love your enemies, and pray for those who persecute you.
MATTHEW 5:43–44

NOVEMBER 11

Imagine that you had a wealthy relative, and one day her attorney called to tell you she had died and left you a million dollars. The money, he added, was now deposited in a bank in your name, and you could draw on it at any time.

You'd act on it, accepting by faith that what the attorney had told you was true, and you were now a millionaire.

In a far greater way God offers us a gift—the gift of salvation in Jesus Christ. Christ has done everything possible to provide it for you; all you must do is receive it.

This is the testimony: God has given us eternal life,
and this life is in his Son. He who has the Son has life.

1 JOHN 5:11–12

FEBRUARY 19

Anyone who has made a commitment to Jesus Christ is something of a rugged individualist. He or she isn't going to live the same way everyone else lives; their goal now is to follow Christ. This may mean being scorned by family or friends, or taking stands for what is right instead of what is popular.

But in other ways the Christian must not be a rugged, independent individualist. Instead, when we come to Christ we become part of a family—the body of Christ, the Church. Instead of being concerned only about ourselves, we become concerned about others in the family of Christ and their needs.

Pity the man who falls and has no one to help him up!
ECCLESIASTES 4:10

NOVEMBER 10

Paul was under arrest, and the Roman governor Felix had full authority either to release him or keep him in jail. Rather than flatter Felix or try to win his favor, however, Paul instead spoke openly to him about Christ. Finally Felix had had enough; he ordered Paul to leave, promising to listen more fully "when I find it convenient."

Hoping for a bribe (which Paul wouldn't give), Felix did send for him repeatedly—but two years later Paul was still in jail, and Felix was still an unbeliever.

Don't wait until a more convenient time to give your life to Christ; the devil will make sure it never happens.

As Paul discoursed on righteousness, self-control and the judgment to come, Felix was afraid and said, "That's enough for now! You may leave. When I find it convenient, I will send for you."
ACTS 24:25

FEBRUARY 20

Why, in the midst of such a busy day, did Jesus insist His disciples leave the crowds to rest and be alone with Him? He knew that the busier they were, the more they needed to make time to rest and be alone with Him. If they didn't, eventually they would hurt both themselves and those they were seeking to help. The same is true of us.

God knows the demands and responsibilities you face—at home, on the job, even in your church. But God also knows you need His wisdom to keep those things in perspective, and you need His strength to get them done rightly.

Then, because so many people were coming and going that they did not even have a chance to eat, he said to [His disciples], "Come with me by yourselves to a quiet place and get some rest."

MARK 6:31

NOVEMBER 9

Is God behind everything that happens to us?

This isn't an easy question to answer. On one hand, God is sovereign, and in ways we can only dimly understand this side of eternity, He is at work behind the scenes. The Psalmist wrote, "He guides me in paths of righteousness for his name's sake" (Psalm 23:3).

But on the other hand, the Bible warns us against assuming that everything that comes our way is from God.

God never leads us to do anything that is contrary to what He has told us in His Word.

Woe to those who call evil good and good evil,
who put darkness for light and light for darkness.

ISAIAH 5:20

FEBRUARY 21

A continual looking forward to the eternal world Jesus will usher in is not a form of escapism or wishful thinking. We Christians look forward with anticipation to Christ's return and spending eternity with Him. The promise of that new world, however, does not mean that we are to leave the present world as it is. If you read history, you will find that the Christians who did the most for the present world were those who thought the most of the next. Only Christians who cease thinking of the next world become ineffective in this one.

"Aim at heaven," said C. S. Lewis, "and you will get earth thrown in. Aim at earth, and you will get neither."

Set your minds on things above, not on earthly things.
COLOSSIANS 3:2

NOVEMBER 8

God wants to help us deal with our anger!

We can't deal with it by ourselves—not fully and finally.
We need God's help, and the first step is to ask Him for it.

Then ask God to help you see others the way He sees them, and love
them as He does. Their wrongdoing may have caused your anger
—but God still loves them. Ask Him to fill you with His love, because
anger and love can't coexist. The Bible says, "Above all, love each other
deeply, because love covers over a multitude of sins" (1 Peter 4:8).

An angry man stirs up dissension,
and a hot-tempered one commits many sins.

PROVERBS 29:22

FEBRUARY 22

Many Christians whose faith and lives testify that they have been converted to Christ do not know the exact day or hour that they left behind the old and the ugly and came to know Him. Whether or not they can remember the specific time, however, they can be sure there was a moment when they crossed over the line from death to life.

That moment comes when we put our faith in certain objective facts —in the work of Christ, His cross, His tomb, and His resurrection. Praise God for calling you to this life-giving faith!

*But to all who did accept him and believe in him
he gave the right to become children of God.*
JOHN 1:12 NCV

NOVEMBER 7

No pastor is perfect, of course; the apostle Paul admitted to the Christians in Corinth that "When I came to you, brothers, I did not come with eloquence or superior wisdom" (1 Corinthians 2:1).

Instead of criticizing your pastor and others who have leadership in your church, show respect for them; God gave them their gifts and their responsibilities. Pray for them also—regularly and sincerely. Encourage them as well, thanking them for what they're doing and expressing appreciation for their service.

Respect those who work hard among you,
who are over you in the Lord.

1 THESSALONIANS 5:12

FEBRUARY 23

It took sixteen hundred years to write. More than thirty authors acting as secretaries for God wrote its sixty-six books. Over those sixteen hundred years, these individual authors wrote the same message, and so unified is the message that the sixty-six books actually comprise one Book.

In the pages of the Bible, the sins of small and great are frankly addressed, the weaknesses of human nature are admitted, and life is presented as it actually is found. The message in every book is straightforward: that message is Jesus Christ. The Bible is primarily concerned with the story of God's redemption of sinful humanity through Jesus Christ.

Righteous are you, O Lord, and your laws are right.
The statutes you have laid down are righteous;
they are fully trustworthy.
PSALM 119:137–138

NOVEMBER 6

One of the habits I have always urged new Christians to develop is the discipline of spending time alone with God every day—reading the Bible, meditating on its truth, and turning to God in prayer. Even if it's only a few minutes at first, nothing can calm our souls more or better prepare us for life's challenges than time spent alone with God.

But the Bible also urges us to walk with God every waking moment.

"Pray continually," Paul urged the Thessalonian Christians (1 Thessalonians 5:17).

On my bed I remember you; I think of you through the watches of the night.

PSALM 63:6

FEBRUARY 24

In Genesis, Jesus is the Seed of the Woman. In Exodus, He is the Passover Lamb. In Leviticus, He is the atoning Sacrifice. In Numbers, the Smitten Rock. In Deuteronomy, the Prophet. In Joshua, the Captain of the Lord's hosts. In Judges, the Deliverer. In Ruth, the Heavenly Kinsman. In Esther, the Advocate. In Job, my Redeemer. In Psalms, my Strength. In Proverbs, my Pattern. In Ecclesiastes, my Goal. In the Song of Solomon, my Satisfier. In the prophets, the Coming Prince of Peace. In the Gospels, He is the Christ who came to seek and to save. In Acts, He is Christ risen. In the epistles, He is Christ exalted. In Revelation, He is Christ returning and reigning.

I am the Alpha and the Omega, the First and the Last,
the Beginning and the End.

REVELATION 22:13

NOVEMBER 5

We can't really put ourselves in God's shoes, of course;
He is far greater than we are. But if you were God, wouldn't you be
tempted to wipe out the human race and blot them from your memory?

But this isn't God's way—and the proof is Jesus Christ. You've heard the
old statement that God hates the sin—but loves the sinner. When Adam
and Eve rebelled against God, He punished them by sending death on the
human race. But He also refused to stamp them out, and even promised
an eventual way of salvation. That way is Jesus Christ.

God demonstrates his own love for us in this:
While we were still sinners, Christ died for us.

ROMANS 5:8

FEBRUARY 25

We Christians ought to carry written on our hearts the solemn truth of how short a time we have to witness for God. Whatever we are going to do for Christ we had better do now.

We had better be sharing our testimony while we have the power. If we are ever to study the Scriptures, if we are ever to spend time in prayer, if we are ever to win souls for Christ, if we are ever to invest our finances for His kingdom, it must be now.

You may not have tomorrow—but you do have today.

As long as it is day, we must do the work of him who sent me. Night is coming, when no one can work.

JOHN 9:4

NOVEMBER 4

It's true: The devil and his demons really do believe in God—and why wouldn't they? They understand that they are engaged in a cosmic battle of titanic proportions, and they know they are up against the Creator of the universe—a truth that makes them shudder. There are no atheists in Hell! But their belief is a far cry from the kind of belief you and I are called to have.

True belief—saving belief—involves not only an intellectual acceptance of certain facts about God and about Jesus. It also involves trust and commitment—trust in Christ as our Savior, and commitment to Him as Lord.

You believe that there is one God. Good!
Even the demons believe that—and shudder.

JAMES 2:19

FEBRUARY 26

Just as the bows and arrows used in warfare centuries ago are useless against today's highly sophisticated weapons, so the carnal weapons that we try to use in spiritual warfare against the devil have no power against his cunning schemes and fierce attacks. Instead, the greatest hindrance to Satan's destructive efforts is our standing strong in the knowledge and fear of the Lord. The greatest roadblock to Satan's work is the Christian who, above all else, lives for God, walks with integrity, is filled with the Spirit, and is obedient to God's truth.

Be self-controlled and alert. Your enemy the devil prowls around like a roaring lion looking for someone to devour. Resist him, standing firm in the faith.

1 PETER 5:8–9

NOVEMBER 3

Life can be hard, and sometimes it leaves us confused, or even angry and bitter. And like Job, you may have told God exactly how you felt. And why not? He already knew your mind and heart, and He doesn't want us to pretend that everything is all right when it isn't. He didn't chastise Job for his honesty; He understood his heartache, just as He understands ours—and He still loved Job, just as He still loves us.

But Job didn't just keep complaining (as we're prone to do). Instead, he turned toward God in faith, and in time, God gave him comfort and peace.

> *I loathe my very life; therefore I will give free rein to my complaint and speak out in the bitterness of my soul."*

JOB 10:1

FEBRUARY 27

The risen Christ commands His followers to "go into all the world and preach the good news" (Mark 16:15). God doesn't promise that obedience will be easy or glamorous or romantic. Oh, I know it's exciting to get on a plane and travel to another land. And perhaps while we're flying God will fill us with His Spirit so that when we reach our destination, we will be prepared to serve Him. But if we are not winning people to Christ here, if we are not witnessing here, if we are not serving Christ here, God can't use us there. We must be faithful here first.

How can they believe in the one of whom they have not heard?
And how can they hear without someone preaching to them?
ROMANS 10:14

NOVEMBER 2

God's moral standards do not change. What He decreed
in the Ten Commandments thousands of years ago is still in force,
and will be to the end of time.

God has given us these standards for another reason: He loves us,
and He wants what is best for us. What happens when an individual
or society ignores these basic moral laws? What happens when lying
and stealing and immorality and murder become the norm?
The result can be summarized in one word: chaos. Thank God that
He cares about us so much that He has told us how to live.

*I tell you the truth, until heaven and earth disappear,
not the smallest letter, not the least stroke of a pen,
will by any means disappear from the Law.*
MATTHEW 5:18

FEBRUARY 28

Shadrach, Meshach, and Abednego were Jewish captives in Babylon—and they refused to worship the golden image set up by King Nebuchadnezzar.

Instead, they risked the tyrant's rage and refused to bow before the idol. They proclaimed, "We take our stand for the living God, even if it means death." Then, calm, self-possessed, joyful, they were condemned and thrown into the fiery furnace, but God was with them and delivered them. God is with His people in the fiery furnaces of life—our times of temptation, trouble, and trial. And people notice the difference His presence makes.

Be faithful, even to the point of death, and I will give you the crown of life.
REVELATION 2:10

NOVEMBER 1

Many today find the idea of reincarnation attractive—the belief that after we die we come back to earth again and again. Some of them have been influenced by other religions; others simply like the thought of enjoying life's pleasures indefinitely.

The Bible, however, is clear: Reincarnation is not true, and the life we are leading now is the only one we will ever live. Once we die, we go into eternity—either to Heaven to be with God forever, or to that place the Bible calls Hell, where we will be eternally separated from God and His blessings.

Man is destined to die once, and after that to face judgment.

HEBREWS 9:27

FEBRUARY 29

Of all the people in the Bible,
Manasseh may have been the most wicked.

So God's judgment fell: the Assyrians captured Jerusalem,
and Manasseh was bound in chains and taken hundreds of miles
away to Babylon. In prison he had time to think, and he began
to pray. In that dungeon this wicked man who only deserved
Hell cried out to God for forgiveness—and God answered.

The Bible teaches that God is a God of mercy. His mercy is so
vast and beyond our comprehension that no matter what sin
we have committed, if we truly repent, God will forgive.

"...The Lord your God is gracious and compassionate.
He will not turn his face from you if you turn to him."

2 CHRONICLES 30:9

OCTOBER 31

The Bible doesn't tell us in detail about Satan and how he works.
After all, our focus should be on God, not on Satan.
(If we concentrate mainly on Satan, we'll become either overly
fearful or overly fascinated—and both are wrong.)

But the Bible does tell us two important truths about Satan,
(whose name means "adversary"). First, he is real, and he will do
everything he can to draw us away from Christ.

Second, Satan is a defeated foe. By His death and resurrection,
Jesus conquered Satan, so by the power of His Holy Spirit in us,
we can stand against him.

*Submit yourselves, then, to God. Resist the devil, and he will
flee from you. Come near to God and he will come near to you.*

JAMES 4:7–8

MARCH 1

If God [weren't perfect], why bother to trust Him?
Why bother to worship Him?

But God isn't like this! God is perfect—absolutely, totally perfect in
all He is and all He does. And because He is perfect, you can trust Him.
You can trust His love, and you can trust His promises. You can trust
Him to guide you, and you can trust Him to be with you even
in life's darkest times. Most of all you can trust Him to save you
through Christ—because His way of salvation is perfect.

As for God, his way is perfect; the word of the Lord is flawless.
PSALM 18:30

OCTOBER 30

The best reason...to give your life to Jesus Christ is because you need Him. You need Him for this life, and you need Him for the life to come. So far in life—whether you realize it or not—you have been following the devil. He promised to give you happiness and peace. But has he kept his promise? No, not at all—nor will he ever keep it. He also promises that you don't need to worry about what will happen to you when you die—which is another lie.

But Christ does not lie. You can depend on His promises—and the greatest promise of all is God's promise of new life in Christ.

*You belong to your father, the devil
...he is a liar and the father of lies.*

JOHN 8:44

MARCH 2

So how do we grow spiritually? We grow through the study of God's Word. We will never grow in grace and in the knowledge of God until the Bible becomes part of our lives every day.

We grow through prayer. We grow as well through our fellowship with other believers. Finally, we grow by witnessing. Just as exercise makes us physically stronger, exercising our faith by sharing it with others makes us spiritually stronger. Are you sharing the story of His love with others?

Grow in the grace and knowledge of our Lord and Savior Jesus Christ.

2 PETER 3:18

OCTOBER 29

The devil is a master at making us question God and His Word. God's command to Adam and Eve had been crystal clear: They could eat of every tree in the Garden—except one. If they ate of it, death would come upon them. But now Satan raises the question: "Did God really say...?" It is the first question in the Bible, and it's significant that it comes from the mouth of the one whose primary goal is to turn us away from God.

But notice: Satan misquoted God! This wasn't what God had told them —as Eve points out in her reply. Twisting Scripture...deceiving us into thinking God is mean-spirited—these are some of Satan's favorite tricks.

[Satan] said to the woman, "Did God really say, 'You must not eat from any tree in the garden'?"

GENESIS 3:1

MARCH 3

The incident occurred when Jesus was twelve. As was their custom every year, Mary and Joseph took Him on the long trip to Jerusalem for Passover, one of the most important Jewish feasts. Afterward they became separated from Him, and when they finally found Him several days later, He was in the Temple listening to those who were teachers of the Old Testament and asking them questions. When Mary and Joseph rebuked Him, he replied, "Why were you searching for me? Didn't you know I had to be in my Father's house?"

If Jesus found it important to be in God's House learning more about God's Word, shouldn't we as well?

Jesus grew in wisdom and stature, and in favor with God and men.

LUKE 2:52

OCTOBER 28

Jesus' first coming passed almost unnoticed: born in a small out-of-the-way town and laid in a manger with only animals and humble shepherds to greet Him on that first night.

How different His second coming will be! Then "every eye will see Him" (Revelation 1:7), and He will come with glory and power to establish His Kingdom of perfect justice and righteousness. No one will dismiss Him as insignificant or unimportant; all will acknowledge Him as King of kings and Lord of lords.

At that time men will see the Son of Man coming in clouds with great power and glory.

MARK 13:26

MARCH 4

Look at the five things Paul lists here which should be part of our character as Christians: compassion, kindness, humility, gentleness, patience. Which is hardest for you? "They're all hard for me," you might be tempted to say—and you're probably right. Every one of them strikes a blow at our natural selfishness. No one exhibited them more completely than our Lord, who was completely self-giving.

But for many of us, patience is the hardest. For one thing, our patience is probably tested every day—even every hour. But patience is also critical, for without it the other four—compassion, kindness, humility, and gentleness—are impossible.

Therefore, as God's chosen people, holy and dearly loved, clothe yourselves with compassion, kindness, humility, gentleness and patience.

COLOSSIANS 3:12

OCTOBER 27

What is the opposite of love?

It isn't hate (although it may take that form). The opposite of love is selfishness. When a husband and wife are concerned only about their own individual desires, the stage is set for conflict.

The Bible gives us another way—the way of Christ. True love, it says, is self-giving, not self-seeking. True love puts the needs of others first. This is what Christ did when He left Heaven's glory and came down to earth for us.

Love is patient, love is kind.... It is not rude, it is not self-seeking, it is not easily angered, it keeps no record of wrongs.

1 CORINTHIANS 13:4–5

MARCH 5

You and I will never be good enough to get into Heaven on our own. The reason is because God is pure and holy, and even one sin—just one— would be enough to keep us out of Heaven. Any and every sin is an offense to God. He does not take our good deeds and bad deeds and weigh them against each other.

That is why we need Christ, for He came into the world to take away our sins. We cannot remove our sins and guilt—but Christ can, because He was the sinless Son of God. When we come by faith to Him, all our sins are transferred to Him, and we are forgiven.

Only those whose names are written in the Lamb's book of life [will enter the glory of heaven].

REVELATION 21:27

OCTOBER 26

Would you like to grow weak? It's not difficult, you know;
all you have to do is stop eating and exercising. And yet no one
in their right mind would willingly do this.

Why, then, do we fail to see the connection between the weakness
of our faith and our lack of spiritual food and exercise? Faith doesn't
grow automatically; it requires spiritual "food" for its nourishment.
It also requires exercise—seeing God work as we put it into action.
And if we don't feed and exercise our souls, we shouldn't be surprised
when our faith grows weaker and weaker.

*Faith comes from hearing the message, and the message
is heard through the word of Christ.*

ROMANS 10:17

MARCH 6

Did you know that the word Christian actually means
"a partisan for Christ"? It means that you have chosen Christ and
are following Him. Partisans are not neutral—they are committed.

Now I want to ask you: "Are you a Christian?" I mean a true Christian,
a real Christian. Many people have a wrong idea of what a Christian is.
They say, "A Christian is a person who prays" or "A Christian
lives by the Golden Rule." But praying or living by the Golden Rule
doesn't make someone a Christian. A person may be sincere,
but that doesn't make him a Christian.

Have you committed yourself to Him as your Lord and Savior?

*Not everyone who says to me, "Lord, Lord," will enter the kingdom
of heaven, but only he who does the will of my Father who is in heaven.*

MATTHEW 7:21

OCTOBER 25

Don't doubt for a moment the devil's existence, and don't doubt for a moment that he is your enemy. Forget the cute cartoon images of an impish figure with a pitchfork and a red suit; he is absolutely malicious and evil, and he has great influence over this world.

He is strong, and he is determined to make you stumble. But we are not defenseless! God has provided us with all the armor we need—armor so strong that Satan and his servants cannot penetrate it. Truth, righteousness, peace, faith, salvation, the Word of God, prayer—every one of these has its part in defeating our adversary.

Put on the full armor of God so that you can take your stand against the devil's schemes.

EPHESIANS 6:11

MARCH 7

The Jewish nation was on the brink of an invasion that would soon destroy it and send most of its inhabitants into exile. And yet few wanted to hear what Ezekiel had to say, for his message warned of God's impending judgment.

Instead they wanted to listen to prophets who declared soothing words, telling them that Ezekiel was wrong and soon the nation would experience peace.

A multitude of talk show gurus promise the same thing. Some may have value—but many are like the false prophets and charm merchants of Ezekiel's day. Don't be misled, and don't be deceived! Instead, build your life on the truth God has given us in His Word.

This is what the Sovereign Lord says: I am against your magic charms with which you ensnare people.

EZEKIEL 13:20

OCTOBER 24

The Bible tells us two important truths about our work.
First, it acknowledges that work—is work! After Adam and Eve sinned,
God cast them out of Eden and declared that "By the sweat of your
brow you will eat your food" (Genesis 3:19 NIV). But the Bible also
tells us that God has given our work to us, and it has dignity and
importance in His eyes. It should in our eyes as well.

Whatever your job—no matter how difficult or enjoyable it is
—"work at it with all your heart, as working for the Lord, not for men."

Whatever you do, work at it with all your heart,
as working for the Lord, not for men.

COLOSSIANS 3:23

MARCH 8

We've all met people who seem to enjoy correcting others and telling them what is wrong with them. Sometimes it's done with an arrogant attitude—the kind that says "I'm better than you, and I know what's wrong with you." Sometimes it's done with an attitude of false humility: "I humbly hope I can help you become a better person." If you're like most of us, however, you probably don't care much for people like this, and (rightly or wrongly) you probably don't listen to their advice.

Instead of criticism, our goal should be to encourage and uplift. Instead of impressing others with ourselves, we want them to be impressed with Christ.

Do not let any unwholesome talk come out of your mouths, but only what is helpful for building others up according to their needs.

EPHESIANS 4:29

OCTOBER 23

You aren't where you are by accident; you are there by God's design. Your country, your city, your family, your job or school—God put you there, and He never does anything without a reason. You are where you are by God's sovereign design, and He wants to use you right where you are.

This world is not our final home; because of what Christ has done for us we have "an inheritance that can never perish, spoil or fade—kept in heaven for you" (1 Peter 1:4 NIV). But in the meantime God calls us to be instruments of His love and justice in an unbelieving world.

Seek the peace and prosperity of the city to which I have carried you.... Pray to the Lord for it."

JEREMIAH 29:7

MARCH 9

The soul requires as much attention as the body. It demands fellowship and communion with God. It demands worship, quietness, and meditation. Unless the soul is fed and exercised daily, it becomes weak and shriveled.

Wise, then, is the person who openly confesses their lack of spiritual wealth and in humility cries out, "God, be merciful to me a sinner!" (Luke 18:13 NKJV). In God's economy, spiritual emptiness comes before filling, and, spiritual poverty before riches. Happiness, Jesus said, comes from admitting our spiritual poverty, and then asking Him to come into our lives.

Blessed are the poor in spirit.
MATTHEW 5:3

OCTOBER 22

God is the same throughout the Bible.

It is true that the Old Testament tells us God is holy and pure,
and He punishes those who rebel against Him. But the New Testament
tells us the same thing. In fact, some of the strongest warnings about
judgment in the Bible come from the lips of Jesus (see Matthew 7:14).

In the same way, the New Testament certainly stresses
God's love and mercy. In fact, it gives us the greatest proof that
God loves us: Jesus laid down His life for our salvation (1 John 3:16).
But the Old Testament also tells us repeatedly about God's love for us.

Jesus Christ is the same yesterday and today and forever.

HEBREWS 13:8

MARCH 10

Being poor in spirit means being aware of our spiritual poverty. Being poor in spirit also means being conscious of our constant dependence on God.

Children depend upon their parents for protection and care. Because of that relationship, children are not poor; but if it weren't for their relationship with their parents, they would be helpless and poor indeed. Dependent children spend little time worrying about meals, clothing, and shelter. They assume—and they have a right to—that all will be provided by their parents. When we come to Christ, we become children of God, and we can trust that our heavenly Father to provide for us.

You are all children of God through faith in Christ Jesus.
GALATIANS 3:26 NLT

OCTOBER 21

Our hearts are sinful. All the things happening in the world that discourage us and cause despair come from the human heart. Our hearts, Jesus said, are a storehouse of evil (Mark 7:21).

Our hearts are far from God (Matthew 15:8). Many of us go to church and outwardly live a good life, but...we are living for ourselves instead of Christ.

Jesus died on the cross to show us the seriousness of our heart condition. He came to cleanse our hearts, to give us a heart-softening picture of God's divine and infinite love, and to woo us to Himself when the world tempts us to stray.

The heart is deceitful above all things
and beyond cure. Who can understand it?

JEREMIAH 17:9

MARCH 11

Should you believe the Bible? Why trust what it says?
One reason is because it tells about real people and real events. It doesn't
consist of stories someone made up (unlike many other ancient books).

Another reason we can trust the Bible is because it was written by
people who actually witnessed what happened. As Peter wrote (who was
himself an eyewitness to Jesus' ministry), "We did not follow cleverly
invented stories...but we were eyewitnesses (2 Peter 1:16).

Most of all, however, we can trust the Bible because it points
us to the most important event in human history: the life, death,
and resurrection of Jesus Christ.

All your words are true; all your righteous laws are eternal.
PSALM 119:160

OCTOBER 20

One reason Christians shouldn't practice astrology is, quite simply, because the Bible tells us not to. Astrology and other forms of fortune-telling were very common in the ancient world, but the Bible writers called them "detestable practices" (Deuteronomy 18:12).

Christians don't follow astrology because we don't need to. God has given us everything we need to know about the future in His Word. Of course, the Bible doesn't tell us what will happen next week or next year; if it did, we would never learn to trust God or seek His guidance.

The heavens declare the glory of God;
the skies proclaim the work of his hands.

PSALM 19:1

MARCH 12

Jesus warned that people "will have to give account on the day of judgment for every careless word they have spoken" (Matthew 12:36). Those are sobering words.

But the answer to reckless words isn't to try to keep silent! Instead, the Bible says, we should seek to do good with our speech: "The tongue of the wise brings healing." Think back over the people who have encouraged or helped you over the years. Weren't they examples of this proverb?

Remember: Jesus Christ wants to be ruler over every part of your life—including your tongue.

Reckless words pierce like a sword,
but the tongue of the wise brings healing.

PROVERBS 12:18

OCTOBER 19

Why is it wrong to tell a lie, even if it doesn't seem to hurt anyone?
One reason—and one that we should take very seriously
—is because God commands us to tell the truth. "You shall not give
false testimony against your neighbor" (Exodus 20:16).

But another reason is because a lie always—without exception—hurts
someone. Or do you honestly want your children, to grow up thinking it
doesn't matter whether or not they tell the truth? Do you honestly want your
unbelieving friends to conclude that Christ doesn't mean anything to you?

Most of all, a lie always hurts the one who tells it.
It makes them less concerned about God's truth.

Each of you must put off falsehood and speak truthfully to his neighbor.

Ephesians 4:25

MARCH 13

One night my wife and I were guests at a dinner with one of America's most brilliant scientists. He told us that he had been an agnostic, but through his study of science he had come to believe that there must be a personal God. So he got a Bible and began to read it—and by reading the Bible he came to know Jesus Christ as his personal Lord and Savior. What is your story? Be ready to share it when the Lord gives you the opportunity. God can use it to point others to Christ's transforming power.

Always be prepared to give an answer to everyone who asks you to give the reason for the hope that you have.

1 PETER 3:15

OCTOBER 18

No matter who we are, what we have done (or haven't done),
God still loves us, and He yearns to welcome every one of us home
—even the black sheep. And although it may startle you,
all of us who call earth our home are black sheep in God's eyes,
for we all have sinned and rebelled against God,
but He has not rejected us—even if we have rejected Him.

Never doubt the depths of God's love—for you,
or for the worst black sheep you know.

I have loved you with an everlasting love.
JEREMIAH 31:3

MARCH 14

We don't need the Bible to tell us (as it does) that there can be pleasure in sin. We know this from our own experience. But the Bible also says that sin's pleasure is only for a season (Hebrews 11:25). Then it's over, leaving us bitter, and finally destroying us. A day of reckoning always comes. No one has ever committed a sin that he or she did not have to pay for.

What sin do you need to leave behind? Repent and return to your Father today. He wants to welcome you home!

You may be sure that your sin will find you out.
NUMBERS 32:23

OCTOBER 17

The Old Testament is God's Word just as much as the
New Testament, and God wants to teach and encourage us through it.
In it, for example, we learn that God made the world—including
you and me. We also learn how sin entered the world, and why
Jesus Christ had to die on the cross for our salvation.

The Old Testament also helps us understand how we should live.
We can learn much from studying the lives of its main
characters—including their failures.

Don't worry about the parts you don't understand. Instead,
ask God to help you learn from the parts you can understand.

Turn my heart toward your statutes and not toward selfish gain.
Turn my eyes away from worthless things; preserve my life according to your word.

PSALM 119:36–37

MARCH 15

It is not a sin to be tempted, for everyone is tempted. The devil tempts, but he can tempt you only so far as God permits—and God always provides a way to escape (1 Corinthians 10:13). The sin is in yielding to temptation, instead of seeking God's power to escape.

When you face temptation, follow Jesus' example. Do what Jesus did. Jesus didn't argue with Satan; Jesus didn't debate with him; Jesus didn't rationalize. Instead He replied, "It is written…". Jesus responded to the enemy's temptation with the simple but strong truth of God's Word, Scripture.

[Take up] the sword of the Spirit, which is the word of God.
EPHESIANS 6:17

OCTOBER 16

Prayer is not something mysterious or secret; prayer is simply talking to God. And God wants you to talk to Him! He loves you, and He has promised to hear you when you pray.

Prayer is possible because Jesus Christ removed the barrier between God and us, a barrier caused by our sins. Sin separates us from God, and because of that, we have no right to come to Him in prayer. But Jesus removed that barrier when He died on the cross for us. When we commit our lives to Christ, God gives us the privilege of approaching "the throne of grace with confidence," (Hebrews 4:16).

This is the confidence we have in approaching God:
that if we ask anything according to his will, he hears us.

1 JOHN 5:14

MARCH 16

As much as we hate to admit it, we are sinners by birth. The Bible is clear: "Surely I was sinful at birth, sinful from the time my mother conceived me" (Psalm 51:5).

We are also sinners by choice. There comes a time—actually it happens several times a day—when we deliberately choose to tell a lie, to steal, to covet, to gossip, to rage.

We are also sinners by practice. The more we do it, the easier it is to practice lust, greed, hate, lying, stealing, or whatever it may be—pride, jealousy, anger.

So we join with Paul...and thank God for sending His Son, our Savior and Deliverer!

Who will rescue me from this body of death? Thanks be to God—through Jesus Christ our Lord!

ROMANS 7:24–25

OCTOBER 15

Ultimately, the Bible says, the devil is the source of all temptation; he is called "the tempter" in Matthew 4:3. But he is able to succeed only because we let him—and we let him succeed because of our own weakness.

This is one reason why we need Christ. Only He can forgive us when we sin, and only He can give us the strength, by the power of His Spirit, to resist temptation. And in His encounter with the devil at the beginning of His ministry He pointed the way to victory: Using the truth of God's Word to counteract Satan's lies.

Jesus said to him, "Away from me, Satan! For it is written: 'Worship the Lord your God, and serve him only.'" Then the devil left him.

MATTHEW 4:10–11

MARCH 17

Saint Augustine was one of the greatest theologians who ever lived. But before he surrendered his heart and his life to Christ, he was a wicked young man, and his besetting sin was lust.

When he was first convicted of his sin, Augustine prayed, "O Lord, make me pure—but not yet." Only when he prayed, "Now, Lord, now. Do it now, Lord," was he forgiven and cleansed.

What besetting sin do you struggle with? Sin is often, if not always, the perversion of something good. In the midst of all our sinning, though, God is willing to forgive us, change us, and give us a new power to overcome that sin.

If we confess our sins, he is faithful and just and will forgive us our sins and purify us from all unrighteousness.

1 JOHN 1:9

OCTOBER 14

How can your faith become stronger? First, be sure of your commitment to Christ. Have you acknowledged your sins to God, and put your faith and trust in Jesus Christ as your Savior and Lord.

Second, build your faith on the truths of God's Word. The Bible is spiritual "food" given to us by God to strengthen our faith. In it, we learn of God's love for us, and also how He wants us to live.

Finally, draw strength from other believers. You need to hear His Word as it is preached and taught.

I pray that out of his glorious riches he may strengthen you.

EPHESIANS 3:16

MARCH 18

If God's Word says, "Fear not," and yet it also says, "Fear," which does it mean? The answer is: both.

Fear is a twofold word. It refers to an emotion marked by dread and anxious concern. But it also means awe and wonder and profound reverence. This latter is the fear that inspires trust and confidence. The Bible calls us to have the latter kind of fear.

When we fear God, we don't cringe before Him like a prisoner robbed of freedom by a ruthless dictator. Our fear causes us to treat God with respect and trust.

Now, O Israel, what does the Lord your God ask of you but to fear the Lord your God, to walk in all his ways, to love him?

DEUTERONOMY 10:12

OCTOBER 13

The first step you need to take to gain victory over sin is to flee from whatever is tempting you. Don't play with it or toy with it in your mind; get as far from it as possible. I have known of people who had to change jobs to keep away from something (or someone) that was tempting them to do wrong! But it was the only way to win.

What step do you need to take to overcome temptation in your life?

Flee the evil desires of youth, and pursue
righteousness, faith, love and peace.

2 TIMOTHY 2:22

MARCH 19

Jesus summed up God's Law with only two commands:
"Love the Lord your God" and "Love your neighbor." And He used
a special, all-encompassing word for love, a word that includes
everyone. We are to love our neighbors, He said, even though they
may have a different color skin, ethnic background, or language; even
though they look different, walk differently, or act differently. We are
also to help our neighbors who are poor. The gospel of Christ has no
meaning unless it is applied to those who are in need.

Love...is not a passive word; it is an action word.
We are to love by our actions.

"Love the Lord your God with all your heart and with all your soul and with
all your strength and with all your mind"; and, "Love your neighbor as yourself."

LUKE 10:27

OCTOBER 12

Why can't we be sinless in this life? Why can't we become perfect? One reason is because sin has weakened us so much that we don't have the strength to overcome its power. Sin is like a deadly disease that infects every part of us: our body, our mind, our emotions, our relationships, our motives—everything.

But when we come to Christ, another spiritual power takes up residence within us: The Holy Spirit. Learn to take sin seriously —be on guard against it resist its tug, fight its power. But most of all learn to take the Holy Spirit seriously, calling on Him to help you overcome sin's power and live a holy and godly life.

What kind of people ought you to be?
You ought to live holy and godly lives.

2 PETER 3:11

MARCH 20

God's call on your life may not be as dramatic as mine was, and the ministry that results from your obedience may not be the same as mine. But none of that takes away from the significance of what you are doing with your life in the service of your King.

William Borden, heir to a large fortune and graduate of Yale, sacrificed everything to go to China as a missionary. He got as far as Egypt and died. Later it was written of him that he had "no reserve, no retreat, no regrets." May you and I also live for Christ with no reserve, no retreat, and no regrets.

There are different kinds of gifts, but the same Spirit.
There are different kinds of service, but the same Lord.
There are different kinds of working, but the same
God works all of them in all men.

1 CORINTHIANS 12:4–6

OCTOBER 11

It is unfortunate when Christians can't get along or even refuse to have anything to do with one another. Not only does this harm our witness to an unbelieving world, but it turns us away from God's priorities for us. Shortly before His death on the cross, Jesus prayed for unity among those who would come to believe in Him. When the world sees Christians fighting, they wonder if the Gospel is really true. Only Satan wins when sincere Christians reject one another.

Do what you can to live at peace with your fellow believers —and join your Lord in praying for the unity of Christ's people, so "that the world may believe" (John 17:21).

May they be brought to complete unity to let the world know that you sent me and have loved them even as you have loved me.

JOHN 17:23

MARCH 21

When we preach Christ crucified and risen, that message has a built-in spiritual power. The Holy Spirit takes the simple message of the cross, with its theme of redemptive love and grace, and infuses it with authority. This supernatural act of God's Spirit breaks down barriers in people's hearts.

So whether you're preaching with actions or words—in your home, neighborhood, or workplace—be sure that you're preaching the Cross. The Spirit will be at work.

*I resolved to know nothing while I was with you
except Jesus Christ and him crucified.*
1 CORINTHIANS 2:2

OCTOBER 10

Angels are just as active today as they were in Bible times. Angels are spiritual beings that seldom assume physical form, which is why we don't see them and are largely unaware of their presence. But I am convinced that when we get to Heaven, we will be amazed to discover how often God's angels intervened to help or protect us. The Bible says that God "will command his angels concerning you to guard you in all your ways" (Psalm 91:11).

Are not all angels ministering spirits sent to serve those who will inherit salvation?

HEBREWS 1:14

MARCH 22

One of our associate evangelists was preaching at a university. One young woman was especially antagonistic. After the lecture she came to him and said, "I don't believe anything you said."

He replied, "I'm sorry that you don't agree, but do you mind if I pray for you?"

She answered, "...I guess it won't do any harm."

He bowed his head and began to pray. She stood looking straight ahead [until she noticed] tears were coming down his cheeks. When he opened his eyes, she herself was in tears. She said, "No one in my entire life has ever shed a tear for me." They sat on a bench and that woman accepted Christ as her Savior.

Dear children, let us not love with words or tongue but with actions and in truth.

1 JOHN 3:18

OCTOBER 9

Have you ever had someone you loved do something that embarrassed or hurt you? Probably. But did you stop loving that person? No! You might have been disappointed, but you kept on loving them.

In a far greater way, God still loves us—even when we disappoint Him or do something wrong. He loves us in the good times, but He also loves us when things aren't going our way and we begin to doubt Him. God's love for us is constant—in the good times and the bad.

Because of the Lord's great love we are not consumed,
for his compassions never fail.

LAMENTATIONS 3:22

MARCH 23

[A] minister went to his medicine shelf and brought back a bottle of strychnine marked "Poison." He said, "...Suppose I take this 'Poison' label off the bottle and put on a label like 'Peppermint Candy.' Can't you see the problem? The milder you make the label, the more dangerous the poison's presence."

It is high time we put a "Poison" label back on the poison of sin. We must to not be afraid to be as plain as the Bible is about the tragic consequences of sin—or about the antidote for that poison: the blood of Christ.

For the wages of sin is death, but the gift of God is eternal life in Christ Jesus our Lord.

ROMANS 6:23

OCTOBER 8

Don't dismiss the Bible because it was written thousands
of years ago. God has not changed...human nature has not changed...
and neither has our need for Christ and His salvation. From Genesis
through Revelation, the Bible points us to Jesus Christ, who was God
in human flesh, sent from Heaven to save us from our sins. It also points
us to God's perfect will for our lives.

Let the Bible's truth become part of your life every day.

*Prophecy never had its origin in the will of man, but men spoke
from God as they were carried along by the Holy Spirit.*

2 PETER 1:21

MARCH 24

The name of Pontius Pilate will be forever linked to...the
final order condemning Jesus to death by crucifixion.

But the name of Pontius Pilate will also stand forever as a prime example
of someone who knew what was right—but failed to do it. He caved in to
the pressures of the crowd and ordered Jesus' death. How often do you cave
in to the pressures of the crowd, seeking the approval of others instead of
the approval of God? Make it your goal to live for Christ and be faithful to
Him, regardless of what the crowd demands.

*Then Pilate announced... "I find no basis for a charge against this man"
.... But with loud shouts they insistently demanded that he be crucified,
and their shouts prevailed.*

LUKE 23:4, 23

OCTOBER 7

We Christians aren't perfect, and we don't become perfect
when we join together in a church. In God's plan, churches should
reflect Jesus Christ, and when church leaders or church members
do wrong, they bring dishonor to His name.

When you come to Christ, commit your life to Him, God accepts you
as an individual, just as you are. And sometimes He draws us closer to
Himself when we reflect on His beauty or enjoy His good gifts.

But when you come to Christ, you also become part of His family.
Every true Christian is now your brother and sister
—and you need each other.

Love the brotherhood of believers.

1 PETER 2:17

MARCH 25

The pride that God loathes is not a healthy self-respect or a legitimate sense of personal dignity. It is the haughty, undue self-esteem out of all proportion to our actual worth. It is the repugnant egotism that is repulsive to both man and God. It is that revolting conceit which swaggers before men and struts in the presence of the Almighty. And God hates it.

What can you do about it? Confess your pride. Humble yourself in the sight of God. Look then at Christ, who "humbled himself and became obedient to death—even death on a cross!" (Philippians 2:8).

The Lord detests all the proud of heart.
Be sure of this: They will not go unpunished.

PROVERBS 16:5

OCTOBER 6

We don't use the word "backsliding" as much as we used to —but the reality is still with us: A seemingly sincere Christian begins to "slide backward" in their faith, returning to their old ways and acting as if Jesus no longer means anything to them.

Why does it happen? Sometimes their faith wasn't real; they had never committed their lives to Jesus Christ in the first place.

But it also happens to believers—and when it does, Satan rejoices. The good news is that God loves even the backslider, and stands ready to forgive. Guard against sliding backward in your faith. Return to God—and He will return to you.

This is what the Lord Almighty says: "Return to me,"
declares the Lord Almighty, "and I will return to you."
ZECHARIAH 1:3

MARCH 26

Anger is one sin that everyone is capable of committing.
Anger brings out the animal nature of human beings. It hinders our
Christian testimony, and causes people to lose the joy of living. Too many
of us excuse our anger by blaming our natural disposition, but anger is sin.

The first step in finding victory over anger is to want to get rid of it.
Next comes confession. Then comes a yielding to God. His Spirit can
tame your tongue and your passions when you surrender your heart
to Jesus. He who calmed the turbulent Sea of Galilee can calm the
tempestuous sea of your anger with His love.

A fool gives full vent to his anger.
PROVERBS 29:11

OCTOBER 5

A woman wrote me recently. "Why didn't God answer us?"
Even if God didn't answer her prayers the way she hoped He would, He
did not ignore them. In fact, He answered her prayers in a far greater
way than she realized—because now her husband is in Heaven, and all
his sickness and pain are over. He has been healed! In the midst of our
tears there still can be joy, because we know that those who die in the
Lord are now with Christ, "which is better by far" (Philippians 1:23).

The body that is sown [in death] in perishable,
it is raised imperishable; it is sown in dishonor, it is raised in glory;
it is sown in weakness, it is raised in power.

1 CORINTHIANS 15:42–43

MARCH 27

Envy dethrones God. Envy destroys our spiritual health, and it takes the joy, happiness, and contentment out of living. Envy becomes a spiritual leprosy, isolating us from both God and other human beings. No wonder God ranks envy on the same level as sexual immorality, idolatry, witchcraft, and drunkenness (see Galatians 5:19–21).

To get rid of this devastating poison, first recognize that you have it. Then confess your sin to God and renounce it. Finally, since envy cannot be overcome in your own strength, open your heart to transforming power of Christ.

A heart at peace gives life to the body, but envy rots the bones.

PROVERBS 14:30

OCTOBER 4

Have you ever asked yourself why God takes anger so seriously and urges us to cast it out of our lives?

One reason is because of what it does to other people. When we lash out at someone in anger, we hurt them and create conflict with them—and that is wrong.

God also hates our anger because of what it does to us. Anger cuts us off from others; no one likes to be around someone who may explode at any moment.

Most of all, anger cuts us off from God, because anger makes us preoccupied with our own problems rather than God's will for our lives.

As churning the milk produces butter, and as twisting the nose produces blood, so stirring up anger produces strife.

PROVERBS 30:33

MARCH 28

Purity is considered smug, but impurity is considered smart
—and the consequences of this vicious sin are played down.
Satan fails to speak of the remorse, the futility, the loneliness,
and the spiritual devastation that go hand in hand with immorality.

Christ can do only one thing with the sin of impurity—and every
other sin. Jesus neither condones sin nor condemns it; He forgives it.
He will also cleanse you and give you victory over your sin. Jesus said to
the immoral woman, "Go now and leave your life of sin" (John 8:11).
He says that to you as well—and He never told anyone to do something
without offering them the power to do it.

*Among you there must not be even a hint of sexual immorality,
or of any kind of impurity…because these are improper for God's holy people.*

EPHESIANS 5:3

OCTOBER 3

Is the Gospel of Jesus Christ complete? Or do we need something else in addition to what the Bible tells us?

Jesus Christ is all we need—and the reason is because He alone was the Son of God, sent from Heaven as God's final sacrifice for our sins. Cults deny this—but the Bible is clear: "Salvation is found in no one else, for there is no other name under heaven given to men by which we must be saved" (Acts 4:12). Thank God for this truth!

Dear friends...[I] urge you to contend for the faith that was once for all entrusted to the saints.

JUDE 3

MARCH 29

Gluttony is a perversion of a natural, God-given appetite.
The gratification of our fleshly appetites is not to receive first
importance in our lives. When we cater to the appetites of the flesh—
when a normal hunger is extended into abnormality so that it harms
the body, dulls the mind, and causes us to neglect the soul
—we become guilty of the sin of gluttony.

When we acknowledge that sin and confess it, Jesus will forgive
the past and provide the power of self-discipline, temperance,
and restraint for the days ahead.

So whether you eat or drink or whatever you do, do it all for the glory of God.
1 CORINTHIANS 10:31

OCTOBER 2

Hagar was a single parent, and she almost gave in to despair.
Perhaps you are in that situation also, or you may know of someone
who is.Forced to flee into the desert with her son, Hagar ran out of
water and felt the end had come. But God had not abandoned her,
and we read that He helped her see a well of water He had provided.
It had been there all along, but Hagar only saw it with God's help.

Being a single parent is very difficult. Don't give in to despair or self-pity,
but look to Jesus Christ every day for the hope and strength you need.

*God opened [Hagar's] eyes and she saw a well of water
…[and] God was with the boy as he grew up.*

GENESIS 21:19–20

MARCH 30

The slothful person is like a piece of driftwood floating effortlessly and heedlessly downstream with the current. It takes no effort, no strength to be lost. Likewise, a drifting, slothful soul is inevitably moving toward an eternity of destruction.

The sin of doing nothing—the sin of omission—is just as dangerous as any sin of action—of commission. You don't have to do anything to be lost: just do nothing. Just be slothful about your soul. Tragically thousands of us Christians are slothful also—when it comes to prayer, worship, reading the Bible, witnessing for Christ, helping neighbors in need, giving to charity, or giving to God's work.

Don't let this happen to you.

The sluggard's craving will be the death of him,
because his hands refuse to work.

PROVERBS 21:25

OCTOBER 1

The Old Testament is just as much God's Word as the New Testament, and God has much to teach us through its pages. "All scripture is given by inspiration of God, and is profitable" (2 Timothy 3:16 KJV). And one of the most important things God wants to teach us from the Old Testament is how not to live.

The Old Testament tells us about some of God's greatest servants—Joseph, Moses, Jeremiah, and so forth—and God has much to teach us from their example. But the Old Testament also is filled with the accounts of men and women who failed God. They, too, are examples, warning us of what happens when we turn aside from following Christ.

Now these things occurred as examples to keep us from setting our hearts on evil things as they did.
1 CORINTHIANS 10:6

MARCH 31

A close relative of covetousness, greed is quite possibly the parent of more evil than any other sin. Greed cheats, robs, murders, and slanders in order to achieve its desires—and each of us is born with greed in our nature.

The Bible teaches that greed is idolatry, because it places things at the center of our lives instead of God. As long as the prodigal son sang the song of "Give me," his lot was misery, want, loneliness, and famine. But when he changed his song to "Forgive me," he found himself in a state of fellowship, comfort, and plenty. What song are you singing?

From the least to the greatest, all are greedy for gain.

JEREMIAH 6:13

SEPTEMBER 30

The world was indeed a perfect place—before Adam and Eve chose to believe Satan's lies instead of God's truth. Adam and Eve had everything they needed, and they walked in perfect harmony with God—until they turned their backs on Him. Suddenly sin —like a deadly cancer—took root in the human heart, and even the plants and animals became ravaged by sin and death.

The Bible tells us, however, that this sin-sick, fallen world won't last forever. At the end of time God will intervene, and the new heaven and new earth He will create will be free from all evil and pain.

God saw all that he had made, and it was very good.

GENESIS 1:31

APRIL 1

Sin must be punished. If God were simply to forgive our sins without judging them, then there would be no justice, no accountability for wrongdoing. God would not be truly holy and just.

But if God were simply to judge us for our sins as we deserve, there would be no hope of salvation for any of us. His love would have failed to provide what we need.

The cross was the only way to resolve the problem of sin. At the cross God's love and justice came together. Jesus took the punishment we deserved, and now we are clothed in His perfect righteousness.

Then Jesus went with his disciples to a place called Gethsemane ...and he began to be sorrowful and troubled.

MATTHEW 26:36-37

Birth is only the beginning for a newborn baby; that child isn't meant to be a baby forever, but to grow and become strong and eventually reach adulthood. The same is true for us. When we first come to Christ we are "spiritual newborns"—but we aren't meant to remain that way. God's plan is for us to grow strong in our faith and become mature in our understanding of God's will.

Are you growing in your faith? If not, why not? Make God's "pure spiritual milk" part of your soul's diet every day.

Like newborn babies, crave pure spiritual milk,
so that by it you may grow up in your salvation.

1 PETER 2:2

APRIL 2

Some skeptics have said that Jesus' agony in Gethsemane was a sign of weakness. They point out that many martyrs, for instance, died without the intense emotional wrestling of Jesus. But it is one thing to die for a cause or for a country. It is quite another to die for an entire world—for all the accumulated sins of generations past and generations to come.

No one ever experienced greater spiritual suffering than Jesus.
His death was a spiritual battle against the powers of darkness,
and His resurrection meant the triumph of God over Satan.
No mere man could defeat Satan. Only Jesus.

Being in anguish, [Jesus] prayed more earnestly,
and his sweat was like drops of blood falling to the ground.

LUKE 22:44

SEPTEMBER 28

Nothing will help us grow spiritually more than spending time alone with God every day, reading His Word and praying. I know our lives are busy today, but time alone with God is essential to our spiritual welfare. Most of us wouldn't think of missing a meal, yet we miss our spiritual "meals" when we neglect God's Word—and we end up spiritually weak.

Many years ago I heard a speaker say something I have never forgotten: "Either sin will keep you from God's Word, or God's Word will keep you from sin." Even five minutes alone with God each day can renew and strengthen your soul.

Your word is a lamp to my feet and a light for my path.
PSALM 119:105

APRIL 3

On that first Easter morning, something happened that had never happened before in the history of the human race—and would never happen again: someone came back from the dead, never to die again....

Jesus' resurrection also tells us that there is life beyond the grave. This world is not all there is; when we die, we continue to live—either in the place of utter darkness the Bible calls Hell or in the place of endless joy the Bible calls Heaven. And now Jesus has opened the way to Heaven for us, by His death and resurrection. Because Jesus rose from the dead, death has been defeated and Heaven awaits us.

I am the resurrection and the life. He who believes in me will live, even though he dies; and whoever lives and believes in me will never die.

JOHN 11:25–26

Do you need to swallow your pride? Do you need to apologize or admit you were wrong about something? Do you need to work to restore your relationship with a brother or sister in Christ—especially if you were the one at fault? Or...do you need to get back into a fellowship of believers?

If so, confess your pride and seek God's wisdom and strength for the future. Let go of your pride—and then patiently wait to see how God will work to restore and change your heart and your life.

Patience is better than pride.

ECCLESIASTES 7:8

APRIL 4

Did you know that the same power that raised Christ from the dead is available to you and me today? The moment we receive Jesus as Savior, the Holy Spirit comes into our hearts. He gives us supernatural power to overcome temptations, to smile through tears, to experience joy despite life's burdens and trials. The Holy Spirit will raise you from the mundane, the monotonous, the hopeless; He will raise you out of your spiritual lifelessness and transform you.

[May you know] his incomparably great power for us who believe. That power is like the working of his mighty strength, which he exerted in Christ when he raised him from the dead.

EPHESIANS 1:19–20

SEPTEMBER 26

The Bible makes it clear that Satan is real, and that he is ultimately behind all the evil that goes on in the world. Before he rebelled against God (long before the human race was created), the world was perfect; sin and evil didn't exist. But now we live in a fallen, twisted, sin-infested world—and Satan is the reason.

But on the other hand, Satan is not all-powerful, nor does he directly cause every bad thing that happens to us.

By His death and resurrection, Jesus triumphed over all the forces of evil—those in our heart and those in the world.

Each one is tempted when, by his own evil desire, he is dragged away and enticed. Then, after desire has conceived, it gives birth to sin.
JAMES 1:14–15

APRIL 5

Why did Jesus willingly die such a violent death? The Bible says He went to the cross for one reason: to become the final and complete sacrifice for our sins. Each of us has sinned; each of us is guilty before God; each of us deserves to die. God is holy and just, and sin must be punished. But Christ became our substitute; He died in our place. He was without sin, but all our sins were placed on Him, and He willingly took the punishment and death we deserve.

He was pierced for our transgressions,
he was crushed for our iniquities;
the punishment that brought us peace was upon him,
and by his wounds we are healed.

ISAIAH 53:5

The Incarnation—God's taking upon Himself our humanity
and becoming a man—is an amazing truth—and one that
gives us a solid foundation for our faith.

Both Jesus and the very first Christians clearly asserted that He was
fully divine, and over the centuries this truth has remained central
to the Christian faith. Long before Jesus' miraculous birth, the Old
Testament foretold that God would enter this world in human form:
"'The virgin will be with child and will give birth to a son, and they
will call him Immanuel'—which means, 'God with us'" (Matthew 1:23).

[Jesus] is the image of the invisible God.

COLOSSIANS 1:15

APRIL 6

When Jesus was put to death, He truly died. The Roman soldiers who nailed Him to the cross attested to that fact when they took His body down and placed it in a tomb. Its entrance was sealed with a huge stone and placed under guard. But that was not the end of the story.

Two days later the tomb was empty, and shortly afterward Jesus appeared numerous times to His followers—as many as five hundred on one occasion. His resurrection proved that Jesus was who He claimed to be, the Son of God, sent from Heaven to save us from our sins.

For what I received I passed on to you as of first importance: that Christ died for our sins according to the Scriptures, that he was buried, that he was raised on the third day according to the Scriptures.

1 CORINTHIANS 15:3–4

SEPTEMBER 24

Which wing of an airplane is more important? Obviously both are equally necessary, and therefore both are equally important.

Which is more important: what we believe about God or what kind of life we live? Again, both are equally necessary, and therefore both are equally important.

In fact, the Bible says that if we claim to believe in Christ but it doesn't make any difference in the way we live, then our faith isn't really genuine. This doesn't mean we must be perfect...but it does warn us about the dangers of a shallow belief in Christ that isn't honest or real.

What good is it, my brothers, if a man claims to have faith but has no deeds? ... Faith by itself, if it is not accompanied by action, is dead.

JAMES 2:14, 17

APRIL 7

Think about the holes children make when they dig in the sand on the seashore. When the waves come in, the holes are swallowed up by the ocean. Similarly, when we know Christ, our physical death is overwhelmed by the love and grace of God. Death is swallowed up in the victory of Christ.

Death is an incident, not an end. It is a transition for a Christian, not a terminus.... We lay aside the outward "tent" of our body, and we inherit "a building from God, a house not made with hands, eternal in the heavens" (2 Corinthians 5:1 NASB).

Our Savior, Christ Jesus... has destroyed death and has brought life and immortality to light through the gospel.
2 TIMOTHY 1:10

Jesus demands to be Master and Lord of every part of your life.
Is He Lord of your mind, of what you think, read, and believe?
Of what you dream about, meditate on, and entertain yourself with?
Is Jesus the Master and Lord of your body? Are you presenting it to
Christ as a living sacrifice? Do your eyes belong to Christ? What about
your ears? Your mouth? Your hands? Your feet? Your sexual urges?
Always ask yourself these questions about your plans: "Can I ask God's
blessing on it? Can I do this to the glory of God? Or will this be
a stumbling block to me or someone else?"

Why do you call me "Lord, Lord," and do not do what I say?
LUKE 6:46

APRIL 8

It has often been pointed out that Jesus lived in a small country and never went beyond its borders. He was so poor that He said He had nowhere to lay His head. His only pocketbook was the mouth of a fish. He rode on another man's beast. He cruised the lake in another man's boat. He was buried in another man's grave. And He had laid aside a royal robe for all this.

He never wrote a book. His recorded words would hardly make a pocket edition. Yet if all the words that have been written about Him were brought together, they would fill a thousand libraries.

Praise be to God and Father of our Lord Jesus Christ, who has blessed us in the heavenly realms with every spiritual blessing in Christ.

EPHESIANS 1:3

SEPTEMBER 22

This verse introduces one of the Bible's great chapters
—what someone has called "The Bible's Hall of Fame."

These great men and women of faith faced discouragement and
doubt the same way we do. But their trust was in God, not their
emotions—and the same should be true of us.

Emotions aren't wrong; God gave them to us, and they are an
important part of life. But our feelings go up and down—and if our
faith is based merely on our feelings, it too will go up and down.
Only when we build our lives on Christ will our faith be stable and strong.

*Now faith is being sure of what we hope for
and certain of what we do not see.*

HEBREWS 11:1

APRIL 9

Why is the Cross an offense?

First, the Cross of Christ is an offense because it condemns the world. It says, "You are sinners"—and we don't like someone pointing out our faults, failures, mistakes, and especially our sins.

The Cross also offends and confuses an unbelieving world because blood was shed, and blood is repulsive. But Christ's blood is the blood of redemption, forgiveness, peace, and reconciliation. By His blood—by His death on the cross—we are released from the guilt of sin and accepted as righteous in God's sight (see Colossians 1:20).

For the message of the cross is foolishness to those who are perishing, but to us who are being saved it is the power of God.

1 CORINTHIANS 1:18

SEPTEMBER 21

From time to time someone writes me who was adopted as a child,
and is now haunted by the idea that they had been rejected by both
of their birth parents, and therefore they must have been unloved and
unlovable. Those feelings have oppressed them most of their lives.

What they have forgotten—and what I always try to point out
to them—is that they weren't unloved and unwanted by their
adoptive parents—not at all. That couple had a choice in the matter
—and they deliberately chose to bring this child into their family.

When you accepted Christ, you were adopted into His family forever.

He chose us in him before the creation of the world
...to be adopted as his sons through Jesus Christ,
in accordance with his pleasure and will.

EPHESIANS 1:4–5

APRIL 10

Paul could have gloried in other aspects of Jesus' life.
He could have gloried in His birth: Jesus was virgin born.
Or in the teachings of Jesus: no one had ever taught like Jesus.
Paul could have gloried in the resurrection of Jesus or in His future
glory when He will return as the victorious and conquering King.

But Paul gloried in the cross. Why? The cross shows the seriousness
of our sin—but it also shows us the immeasurable love of God.
Furthermore, the cross is the only way of salvation. And the cross
gives a new purpose to life. Once you have been to the cross,
you will never be the same.

God forbid that I should glory, save in the cross of our Lord Jesus Christ.
GALATIANS 6:14 KJV

SEPTEMBER 20

A life without God is like a boat without an anchor.
But God didn't intend for our lives to be this way. And when we
come to know Christ, He brings calm to our chaos and direction to
our drifting. It doesn't necessarily happen overnight—but as we learn
to live by the principles He has given us in His Word, we leave the past
behind and discover the peace He alone can give. Thank God for doing
this in your life—and pray for your friends who do not yet know Christ,
that they may find in Him the stability and peace they seek.

But the wicked are like the tossing sea, which cannot rest,
whose waves cast up mire and mud. "There is no peace,"
says my God, "for the wicked."

ISAIAH 57:20–21

APRIL 11

If you have truly asked Christ to come into your life, you can be confident that the Holy Spirit resides in you—whether or not you feel His presence. The Bible says, "For you...received the Spirit of sonship" (Romans 8:15).

Even though the Spirit lives within us, however, we must yield our lives to Him every day because our old nature is still present. Furthermore, Satan will try to tempt us and convince us we must fight our spiritual battles alone.

Do you not know that your body is a temple of the Holy Spirit, who is in you, whom you have received from God?
1 CORINTHIANS 6:19

SEPTEMBER 19

In reality...we often don't know why God permits certain things to happen to us. We do know that evil is real, and we live in a world that is ravaged by sickness and death and sorrow—a world that isn't the way God intended it to be. Some day Christ's victory will be complete and all this will be changed—but not yet. In the meantime, put your faith and hope in Christ. He knows what it is to suffer; he went to the cross for us. And because He did, we have hope even in the midst of life's darkest hours.

If only my anguish could be weighed and all my misery be placed on the scales! It would surely outweigh the sand of the seas.

JOB 6:2–3

APRIL 12

Generosity doesn't come naturally to most of us—not the kind of generosity the Bible urges us to have. Most of us will gladly give if we think the cause is worthy and we feel we can afford it. But the Bible urges us to go beyond that: to give sacrificially to God's work.

God's work demands prayer, and dedication, and vision, and reliance on the Holy Spirit. But it also requires our financial resources.

Never forget: Everything you have has been given to you by God.

Give, and it will be given to you. A good measure, pressed down, shaken together and running over, will be poured into your lap. For with the measure you use, it will be measured to you.

LUKE 6:38

SEPTEMBER 18

Love isn't just a feeling; love must be expressed in action. If it isn't, we won't have any reason to believe it even exists in someone's life, no matter how much they claim it does.

Nor is God's love just a vague feeling or sentimental emotion hidden in His heart. God's love is real—and we know it because He demonstrated it to us. He put His love into action! Do you want to know if God loves you? Here is the proof: Jesus Christ left Heaven's glory and came down to this sin-infested earth to die for you.

This is how God showed his love among us: He sent his one and only Son into the world that we might live through him.

1 JOHN 4:9

APRIL 13

When someone complains to you about the church always
asking for money, gently remind them of two things.

First, invite them to consider what most churches actually do with the
money they collect. Almost without exception they use it to reach out to
others, seeking—with God's help—to make this world a better place.
Second, encourage them to look beyond their superficial impressions
and ideas about Jesus, and discover what He is really like—by turning to
the New Testament Gospels and letting Jesus speak for Himself.

Now about the collection for God's people.... On the first day of every week,
each one of you should set aside a sum of money in keeping with his income.

1 CORINTHIANS 16:1–2

SEPTEMBER 17

One of the Bible's greatest truths is that our lives can be different.
No matter what our past has been, Christ stands ready to forgive and
cleanse us—and then to make us new. Only Christ can bring hope to lives
that have been turned into ashes by the assaults of our enemy, Satan.
And He doesn't just restore us to what we once were; He gives us "a crown
of beauty"—the beauty of forgiveness, and the beauty of hope and joy
and peace. Who around you is experiencing the ashes of a shattered life?
Pray for them, and ask God to use you to point them to Christ.

The Lord has anointed me...to bestow on them
a crown of beauty instead of ashes.
ISAIAH 61:1, 3

APRIL 14

Money can all too easily become our master instead of our servant. Once we put Christ first in our life, however, we can ask Him to help us trust Him for our needs. Our heavenly Father knows we need clothes, food, and a place to live, so we don't need to worry. That may seem impossible, but God will give us His peace as we learn to trust Him.

We also need to deal with our finances responsibly— following a realistic budget; developing a plan to pay off debt; even cutting up our credit cards if necessary.

Don't become a slave to money, but learn to trust God in everything.

*Do not worry about your life, what you will eat or drink....
Your heavenly father knows that you need them."*

MATTHEW 6:25, 32

SEPTEMBER 16

As they grow older our children become responsible for the decisions they make in life; parents shouldn't take upon themselves all the blame if those decisions are bad. But our failures do have an impact on them, making them more open to foolish or evil ways. Harsh, unreasonable discipline...neglect...favoritism...failure to express love... being too busy to give them any attention...failing to teach them the difference between right and wrong...all these and more can "embitter your children" so that "they will become discouraged."

Don't let this happen in your family. And if it has, ask God to forgive you and help you reverse it as much as possible.

Fathers, do not embitter your children, or they will become discouraged.
COLOSSIANS 3:21

APRIL 15

Cheating of any kind will always keep you wondering if you'll be discovered. You won't like the feeling that comes with knowing you lack integrity and are dishonest.

If we cheat, we are disobeying God. In His eyes, failing to pay the taxes we owe is little different from stealing from an individual. Furthermore, if we fail to pay the taxes we owe, honest citizens will have to make up the shortfall.

If cheating of any kind enters our mind, we need to ask ourselves why we would even consider it. Is money too important to us? Is greed ruling us? Whatever it is, confess it and put Christ first in your life.

Give everyone what you owe him: If you owe taxes,
pay taxes; if revenue, then revenue.

ROMANS 13:7

SEPTEMBER 15

When we first glimpse the apostle Paul in the Bible he was called Saul—and his mission in life was to stamp out the Christian faith. But all that changed when he met the risen Lord Jesus Christ on the road to Damascus.

What made him change? First, he became absolutely convinced that the Gospel was true. Jesus Christ was no imposter; He was the risen Son of God, sent from Heaven to save us from our sins.

He began to see people the way God sees them. He now saw them in their lostness and confusion—and also as those for whom Christ died.

So from now on we regard no one from a worldly point of view.

2 CORINTHIANS 5:16

APRIL 16

We can pray all day long. We can go to church every week.
We can read our Bible through a thousand times—but if we are
robbing God, we will be miserable and spiritually dry.

Do you think you can rob God but have victory in your life?
It cannot be done. There is no victory if we aren't giving a
portion of our income to the Lord.

The basis of our giving is the tithe—one-tenth of your
income—is God's (see Malachi 3:10). It's God's rule,
and I believe it is still valid today.

*A poor widow came and put in two very small copper coins....
Jesus said, "I tell you the truth, this poor widow has put more into
the treasury than all the others.... She, out of her poverty,
put in everything—all she had to live on."*

MARK 12:42–44

SEPTEMBER 14

The Bible urges us to...find our hope in God—not in our circumstances, or our natural optimism (or pessimism), or our family or friends—but from God.

How is this possible? It happens only when we realize how much God loves us—a love so deep that His Son was willing to give His life for us. It happens too when we realize that this life is not all, but ahead of us is Heaven if we know Christ. Is your hope in Him—both for this life and the life to come?

Why are you downcast, O my soul?
Why so disturbed within me?
Put your hope in God.

PSALM 42:5

APRIL 17

Year after year we have seen thousands of men, women, and young people receive Christ as Savior throughout the world. People with problems, burdens, and sins have committed their lives to Jesus, and seen a light in their eyes and a glow on their faces as they are transformed by the Spirit of God. When Christ takes up residence in their hearts, they become new creations in Him.

Today, as always, many people think they can manage without God. They may manage economically, intellectually, and even socially. But down inside they have a spiritual void that can be filled only by Jesus Christ.

For to me, to live is Christ.
PHILIPPIANS 1:21

SEPTEMBER 13

You can't solve everything—but don't let that keep you from obeying the Bible's injunction to do good to everyone you can, as God gives you opportunity. It may be by supporting the work your church is doing in your community, or by sending money to an international Christian humanitarian aid organization. Or it may be through helping a single parent who lives near you...or tutoring in a local school...or simply being a friend to someone who is going through hard times.

Jesus said, "Whatever you did for one of the least of these brothers of mine, you did for me" (Matthew 25:40).

As we have opportunity, let us do good to all people.
GALATIANS 6:10

APRIL 18

What giants are you facing? The giant of peer pressure? Of different ideologies and philosophies fighting for control of your life? What about giants like social injustice, moral deterioration, or crime? Or maybe the giant of fear, joblessness, broken relationships, or family conflict?

Goliath had David out-armed and out-experienced. Goliath was a great warrior; David was not. His only weapon was a slingshot —and a deep dependence on God And God gave him victory.

Everyone has problems, and Christ wants to help you face yours—if you will let Him.

David said to the Philistine, "You come against me with sword and spear and javelin, but I come against you in the name of the Lord."

1 Samuel 17:45

SEPTEMBER 12

You've probably had your doctor take a little rubber hammer and tap you on the knees—and if your reflexes are good, your lower leg responded with a gentle kick. That reflexive action occurs automatically, and it's the same every time that nerve gets hit.

But how do you respond when troubles hit you?
What is your automatic reflexive action then?
Panic? Anger? Depression? Confusion? All of these?

James in these verses reminds us what our reflexive action should be: turning to God in prayer.

Is any one of you in trouble? He should pray....
The prayer of a righteous man is powerful and effective.
JAMES 5:13, 16

APRIL 19

Jesus talked about two men who were building houses. One built his house on a solid rock foundation—and when the storms came, his house stood. The other man built his house on sand —and when the storms came, his house crumbled and fell.

Many people today live in homes built on sand. Lacking the right foundation, their family is in trouble. What about you? When the floods of sorrow, the waves of temptation, and the gales of adversity come, will your home stand?

Make Jesus Christ the foundation of your home—and your life.

Whoever comes to Me, and hears My sayings and does them...
is like a man building a house, who dug deep and laid
the foundation on the rock.

LUKE 6:47–48 NKJV

SEPTEMBER 11

I have asked myself hundreds of times why God sometimes allows evil to flourish—and I don't have the full answer. Evil is real, however, and we ignore it at our peril. Evil is so real that it cost God's Son His life.

But I do know this: Even in life's darkest hours, "God is our refuge and our strength". Not money, not military might, not diplomacy, not human cleverness—but God. As you reflect on what happened on that September 11, is God your refuge and strength? He can be, as you open your heart and life to Jesus Christ.

God is our refuge and strength, an ever-present help in trouble. Therefore we will not fear, though the earth give way and the mountains fall into the heart of the sea.

PSALM 46:1–2

APRIL 20

God has His seven wonders.

The first is the wonder of God's love. The Almighty God,
the Creator of the whole universe, loves you and is interested in you as
if you were the only person who ever lived. Even when we sin against
Him, He still wants to put His arms around us and say, "I love you."

The second is the wonder of God coming to live among us.
God became a man—and that man was Jesus.

The third is the wonder of the Cross. Jesus died for you and for me.
Far more than His excruciatingly painful physical death, He suffered
spiritually when God laid on Him your sins and mine.

Because your love is better than life, my lips will glorify you.
I will praise you as long as I live.

PSALM 63:3–4

SEPTEMBER 10

Think of all the advancements in medicine, communications, and technology the human race has made in the last century or so. We should be grateful that God has given us the ability to make this kind of progress.

But now also think of the tragic fact that these same centuries have seen the most devastating wars in human history. In spite of our accomplishments, we humans are still a painful mixture of good and bad, love and hate, joy and sorrow. We have the ability to reach the moon, but we can also destroy millions with the touch of a button.

Only He can make us new; only He can change our hearts and make us more like Himself.

He who was seated on the throne said, "I am making everything new!"

REVELATION 21:5

APRIL 21

The fourth of God's seven wonders is the wonder of conversion.
The word conversion means "to change, to turn." You cannot convert
yourself: you have to have God help you repent.

The fifth wonder is the gift of peace and joy that Christ gives.
God's wondrous love and the gracious forgiveness He offers
through Jesus Christ bring peace and joy.

The sixth wonder is God's plan for the future.
I look forward to that day when He will return.

The seventh wonder of God is your own commitment to Jesus Christ.

*Here I am! I stand at the door and knock. If anyone hears my voice
and opens the door, I will come in and eat with him, and he with me.*

REVELATION 3:20

SEPTEMBER 9

[Many] go through life without ever knowing
God or giving Him His rightful place.

What is the problem? Almost always, I've discovered, they have
made no effort to seek God or find His answer to their problems.
Instead of actively seeking Him, they passively expect Him to come to
their aid without any effort on their part. They ignore Jesus' words:
"Ask and it will be given to you; seek and you will find" (Matthew 7:7).
If you have never trusted Christ for your salvation, don't sit back
and wait for a better time to accept Him; it may never come.
Commit it to God and seek His will without delay.

Seek the Lord while he may be found; call on him while he is near.

ISAIAH 55:6

APRIL 22

A Christian is a person who has made a choice.
We have to choose—just as Adam and Eve did in the Garden of Eden
—to obey God or rebel against Him. We make that choice initially
when we commit our lives to Christ, but we also make that choice day
by day, moment by moment. A Christian is a person whose life has been
changed. That transformation is the work of the Holy Spirit.

A Christian is a person who has accepted a challenge.
The challenge is Jesus' call to deny self—our own selfish ambitions,
our own selfish sinful pleasures—and take up our cross.

*If anyone would come after me, he must deny himself
and take up his cross and follow me.*

MATTHEW 16:24

SEPTEMBER 8

David said he "waited patiently" for God to act—and sometimes that's hard for us to do. But in time God did answer, and God lifted him out of the mire and put his feet on a rock—a picture of what happens when we give our lives to Jesus Christ. He alone is the solid, unshakeable rock on which to build our lives (see 1 Peter 2:6–8).

If you're in a "pit" right now, don't give up. Instead, turn to Christ and find in Him the solid foundation you need.

I waited patiently for the Lord; he turned to me and heard my cry.
He lifted me out of the slimy pit, out of the mud and mire;
he set my feet on a rock.

PSALM 40:1–2

APRIL 23

Whatever gift we have and whatever opportunities may open up to us are from God. We cannot take any credit or glory for ourselves. This understanding will save us from discouragement and the temptation to give up, because we know our calling is not from man but from God. Some are called to be evangelists—but every Christian is called to the work of evangelism, for every Christian is called to tell others about Christ and what He has done for them.

Yet when I preach the gospel, I cannot boast, for I am compelled to preach. Woe to me if I do not preach the gospel!

1 CORINTHIANS 9:16

SEPTEMBER 7

We will never be completely free from sin in this life.
Although Jesus Christ came to live within us by His Spirit when
we gave our lives to Him, our old sinful nature still resides within us,
and as long as we live it will keep trying to assert itself.

But that must not keep us from pursuing perfection! To put it
another way, that must not keep us from battling sin and embracing
righteousness. God's will is that we would become more and more like
Christ—more like Him in our purity, our love, our service.

*Not that I have already obtained all this, or have already been made perfect,
but I press on to take hold of that for which Christ Jesus took hold of me.
Brothers, I do not consider myself yet to have taken hold of it. But one thing I do:
Forgetting what is behind and straining toward what is ahead.*

PHILIPPIANS 3:12–13

APRIL 24

When Israel was entering the Promised Land, the two tribes
of Reuben and Gad saw that the already-conquered territory on
the east side of the Jordan was good for their herds and flocks.
Thinking only of themselves...they approached Moses with a request:
"Let this land be given to your servants as our possession.
Do not make us cross the Jordan." (Numbers 32:5).

Moses was an old man, but his eyes blazed, his jaw set, anger
came to his face. Moses said, "Shall your countrymen go to war while
you sit here?... [If so,] you may be sure your sin will find you out"
(Numbers 32:6, 23). Over the years his words proved to be true.

*Each of you should look not only to your own interests,
but also to the interests of others.*

PHILIPPIANS 2:4

SEPTEMBER 6

When we attempt to do God's work in our own strength instead of God's strength, we will fail. Only when we acknowledge our weakness and look to the Holy Spirit for the wisdom and strength we need will God bless our efforts.

How will you do what needs to be done? Yes, you'll study and work diligently; trusting God for the outcome doesn't mean we sit back and do nothing. But only God can work in the hearts of those you are seeking to help. Confess your weakness to Him and trust Him to work through you—today and always.

For when I am weak, then I am strong.
2 CORINTHIANS 12:10

APRIL 25

The Bible is filled with promises of that coming day of glory.
Its pages indicate that when Christ returns, the world will not be
expecting Him. Just as the people in Noah's day did not believe that a
flood was coming, multitudes today do not believe that God's judgment
is coming. The flood did come, though, and so will His judgment.

Jesus calls us who know Him to wait in expectation. Our hands
should be busy with His work—but our eyes should be looking up.
May your watching for Jesus make you even more active in His service!

Keep watch, because you do not know on what day your Lord will come.
MATTHEW 24:42

SEPTEMBER 5

One of your goals as a parent is to work yourself out of a job. Someday your children will leave home—and a major part of your responsibility is to prepare them for that day. From learning to brush their teeth and tie their shoes to helping with their homework and teaching them to make wise decisions, your goal is to prepare them for the day when you won't be there.

But what about their spiritual foundations? Have they learned from you what it means to walk with Christ every day? Have you taught them to pray, and to love the Bible and live by its truths? Have you encouraged them to give their lives to Jesus Christ?

Impress [these commandments] on your children. Talk about them when you sit at home and when you walk along the road, when you lie down and when you get up.

DEUTERONOMY 6:7

APRIL 26

We are to serve God alone. Whatever our heart clings to is our "god," and when we cling to anything or anyone other than God we are guilty of idolatry. God alone must be first in our heart and our life. Next, we are to avoid anything that excludes or obscures the divine nature of God. We are also to honor His name and enter His presence with reverence and respect. In addition, we are to set aside one day in seven for rest and the worship of God.

And God spoke all these words: "I am the Lord your God, who brought you out of Egypt, out of the land of slavery."

EXODUS 20:1–2

Think of all the people Jesus dealt with during His ministry. Some were society's rejects—the woman caught in adultery, lepers, despised Samaritans, the criminals on the cross. Others were powerful and sophisticated—Nicodemus, Pilate, the Pharisees. They covered the whole social spectrum—but they all needed the Savior; they all were headed toward death and eternity; they all were the objects of His love. Not everyone Jesus tried to turn back from the brink of destruction responded—nor will they with us. But that didn't keep Jesus from trying—nor must it us.

Remember this: Whoever turns a sinner from the error of his way will save him from death and cover over a multitude of sins.

JAMES 5:20

APRIL 27

Christ...will come back. Jesus said that only the Father in heaven knows exactly when—and this should keep us from wild speculations. But Jesus did say that we should watch for certain signs.

We should, for instance, be on guard against false Christs and false prophets. Scripture also teaches that there will be "wars and rumors of war" (Matthew 24:6), as well as unprecedented natural disasters. Christians will be persecuted for their faith.

Another sign of Christ's return will be that hearts once passionate for Jesus will become cold toward Him. This loss of fervent love will contribute to a breakdown of morals, another sign the end is near.

This gospel of the kingdom will be preached in the whole world as a testimony to all nations, and then the end will come.

MATTHEW 24:14

SEPTEMBER 3

Jesus Christ died to save people from even the most remote corner
of the world—people you and I will never know during our lifetimes,
but people we will be with in Heaven forever. God's plan is universal!
No tribe, no language group, no nation is beyond the scope of His love.
Not everyone is called of God to be a missionary or evangelist.
But if you know Christ, you are a partner in His "grand design"
to call men and women from every part of the world to Himself.
By your prayers, your giving, your faithful witness, and your service,
you can have an impact for the Gospel far beyond your homeland.

*And they sang [to Jesus] a new song: "You are worthy
...because you were slain, and with your blood you purchased men
for God from every tribe and language and people and nation."*

REVELATION 5:9

APRIL 28

Observe carefully the prayer life of Jesus, and notice the earnestness with which He prayed. In Gethsemane He cried out with a loud voice, and in the intensity of His supplication He fell headlong on the damp ground and pleaded before His Father until "his sweat was like drops of blood falling to the ground" (Luke 22:44). Too often—and in very sharp contrast—you and I use petty petitions, oratorical exercises, and the same words we have used for years rather than the cries of our inmost being.

Also, too often when we pray, our thoughts roam. We insult God by speaking to Him with our lips while our minds and hearts are far from Him.

When you pray, do not keep on babbling like pagans.
MATTHEW 6:7

SEPTEMBER 2

To ask God to search out the darkest, most secret corners
of our minds and hearts takes courage.

And yet what happens if we aren't willing to do this? Then the sins we
know about remain unconfessed, and our fellowship with God remains
cold and distant. Perhaps more important, the hidden sins we may not
even realize we have—sins like pride, suppressed anger, lack of love,
jealousy, a secret yearning for recognition—remain firmly in place,
manipulating us and eventually destroying us.

Have the courage to pray this prayer. And whatever God
reveals, confess it, repent of it, and ask Christ to replace it
with His purity and love.

*Search me, O God, and know my heart; test me and know
my anxious thoughts. See if there is any offensive way in me.*

PSALM 139:23–24

APRIL 29

Jesus teaches...the victorious assurance that God answers every true petition (although not always the way we wish He would). We need to trust in the promise of John 15:7 and in the complementary intercession of the Holy Spirit (Romans 8:27).

We also need to remember that with God nothing is impossible. No task is too arduous, no problem too difficult, no burden too heavy for Him. Do not, however, put your will above His. Do not insist on your way. And don't expect an immediate answer to come in exactly the way, the place, and the manner that you are seeking. Rather, learn to pray as Jesus Himself prayed.

*If you remain in me and my words remain in you,
ask whatever you wish, and it will be given you.*

JOHN 15:7

SEPTEMBER 1

Do you tend to downplay the work you do? "I'm only a housewife ... I'm just a plumber...I simply teach school.... If God gave you that skill, and you are where He wants you to be, then your work is valuable and significant in His sight.

One other thought for you to ponder: What kind of a carpenter do you suppose Jesus was? Did the doors fall off His cabinets? Do you suppose He took shortcuts, or did just barely enough to get by? No, of course not. The Bible says, "Whatever you do, work at it with all your heart, as working for the Lord, not for men" (Colossians 3:23).

Every skilled person to whom the Lord has given skill and ability ...[is] to do the work just as the Lord has commanded.

EXODUS 36:1

APRIL 30

In this world all of us have trials and tribulations, and each one is an opportunity to pray. But far too often we Christians close our conversation with someone who is struggling with "I'll pray for you" —and, sadly, that's the last of it. We need to be true to our word; we need to live according to the Golden Rule and actually pray for our brothers and sisters the way we would want them to pray for us. But the blessing of such prayer isn't just for the other person.

Far be it from me that I should sin against the Lord by failing to pray for you.
1 Samuel 12:23

AUGUST 31

When we go down a wrong path in life, God grieves over our foolishness, because He knows we are only hurting ourselves. He also knows that this is our natural tendency, because we —like sheep—easily wander and stray from the only Shepherd who can guide us and keep us safe.

What decisions are you facing? Don't rely only on your own wisdom, or even on the wisdom of others. Instead, seek God's will, and ask Him to guide you and show you His will. Remember: His way is always best—always.

We all, like sheep, have gone astray,
each of us has turned to his own way.

ISAIAH 53:6

MAY 1

Some people lose almost all sense of right and wrong—and when that happens the results are always tragic. This is one reason why Christians need to take a stand for what is right and not let evil go unchallenged.

During this first week in May, many people will celebrate an annual Day of Prayer, praying especially for our world and its leaders —its politicians, trendsetters, media powers, athletes, and others in a position of influence. Pray that they may use their influence for good and not for evil. Remember: God is sovereign and is still at work, and He alone is our hope for a better world.

I urge, then, first of all, that requests, prayers, intercession and thanksgiving be made for everyone—for kings and all those in authority, that we may live peaceful and quiet lives in all godliness and holiness.

1 TIMOTHY 2:1–2

AUGUST 30

We've all been hurt by the words of others. Often—perhaps more often than we realize—what was said was simply spoken thoughtlessly or carelessly. But sometimes it wasn't; those words were meant to sting—and they did.

Either way, when others criticize us or say something hurtful or insensitive, our first reaction should be to ask ourselves if there is any truth in what they say. If so, we need to be honest with ourselves, and ask God to help us correct it. But even if those words were spoken maliciously, we need to turn our hurts over the God and ask Him to help us respond with forgiveness and grace.

They sharpen their tongues like swords and
aim their words like deadly arrows.

PSALM 64:3

MAY 2

If God already knows our needs, why pray? Perhaps this question has even kept you from praying—but in reality it should make us pray more.

If you are a parent, do you discourage your children from coming to you with their requests—even if you already know what they want? No, of course not. You love them, and you take delight in listening to them. Even if you say no to their requests, it's because you know better than they do what is best for them.

God, our heavenly Father, loves us, His children —and one of our greatest privileges is coming to Him in prayer.

Your Father knows what you need before you ask him.

MATTHEW 6:8

AUGUST 29

It's natural for us to shrink back from any kind of trial; we all wish we could be free of problems and instead live a life of peace and serenity all our days. But life isn't like this, and we all know that it can radically change even in a matter of seconds. The real question is how we will react. Will we react in anger or despair? Will we lash out in hatred or revenge? Or will turn to God in faith and seek His help?

Consider it pure joy, my brothers, whenever you face trials of many kinds, because you know that the testing of your faith develops perseverance.

JAMES 1:2–3

MAY 3

In spite of His hectic public ministry,
Jesus was never too hurried to spend hours in prayer.

By contrast, how quickly and carelessly we pray (if we pray at all).
In the morning we hastily ask for His blessing on our day,
then say good-bye to God for the rest of the day until we rush through
a few closing thoughts at night. This is not what Jesus modeled.
Jesus prayed deeply and repeatedly. He spent entire nights in
fervent appeal to God. How different is our pattern of prayer!

He went up on a mountainside by himself to pray.
MATTHEW 14:23

AUGUST 28

Ultimately our lives are in God's hands; even the next breath
you take is a gift from Him. If He were to withdraw His hand from you,
your life would end—despite the most strenuous efforts of your doctors.

What difference should this make? First, it should remind us of our
dependence on God. All too often we assume that our lives and our
futures are in our hands. But they aren't; they are in His hands.

But this should also remind us that each day is a gift
from God—a gift to be used wisely, joyfully, and for His glory.

*No man has power over the wind to contain it;
so no one has power over the day of his death.*

ECCLESIASTES 8:8

MAY 4

God isn't limited! He isn't like a computer without enough memory.
God is infinite in His knowledge and wisdom. Since He created this
universe—right down to the smallest subatomic particle—isn't He able
to know every detail of what goes on in the world? Of course!
[One] reason to pray is because God loves us. He is more concerned
about you and about those you love than you are. As Jesus said,
"Are not two sparrows sold for a penny? Yet not one of them will fall to
the ground apart from the will of your Father.... So don't be afraid;
you are worth more than many sparrows" (Matthew 10:29–30).

So pray with confidence to your great God!

Let us then approach the throne of grace with confidence.
HEBREWS 4:16

AUGUST 27

God not only knows what is going on in your life right now, but He knew all about you even before you were born. In fact, He gave you life and put you on this earth. You are not here by accident; you are here by His design!

The same is true of every human being; every person on this earth (even those not yet born) is important in the eyes of God. Don't ever scorn someone because they are different from you, or ignore them when they suffer. God calls them valuable—so valuable that His Son gave His life for them.

Before I formed you in the womb I knew you, before you were born I set you apart; I appointed you as a prophet to the nations.

JEREMIAH 1:5

MAY 5

Do you know why we often close our prayers with the phrase in Jesus' name? Those words remind us that Jesus has opened the door to Heaven for us, and we can approach God only because of what He has done for us. But this phrase isn't a magic formula we add in order to make God answer our prayers. God answers our prayers solely because of Christ.

God knows what is best for us. When you pray, therefore, seek God's will. Thank God for the privilege of prayer, and make it part of your life everyday.

We have peace with God through our Lord Jesus Christ, through whom we have gained access by faith into this grace.

ROMANS 5:1–2

AUGUST 26

It's easy to become cynical about government or feel that our vote is insignificant. But what would happen if everyone had his attitude? What kind of leadership would we likely get then? We need leaders who are men and women of integrity and wisdom, and we should thank God that we live in a country where we have the privilege of choosing our leaders. We must never take that responsibility lightly.

The Bible tells us to pray for "all those in authority, that we may live peaceful and quiet lives in all godliness and holiness" (1 Timothy 2:2).

Righteousness exalts a nation, but sin is a disgrace to any people.
PROVERBS 14:34

MAY 6

The desire for peace is universal. But simply telling people to stop fighting and love each other isn't the solution for the tension, discord, and violence that exist around the globe. Diplomats and leaders have tried to do this for centuries, yet world history is filled with wars and conflicts.

The problem lies within the human heart; by nature we are selfish and greedy. Even leaders aren't exempt from these sins. Even when we want peace, it often eludes us because of our greed or anger or jealousy. Only God can change the human heart, and that is why our greatest need is spiritual renewal. Pray today for our world and its leaders.

Will you not revive us again, that your people may rejoice in you?
PSALM 85:6

AUGUST 25

One of life's hardest lessons is that we cannot turn back the clock and change something we've already done. When we make a wrong decision or act foolishly, we have to live with the consequences, bitter as they may be. In biblical terms, we must reap what we have sown.

Then why bother to ask for God's forgiveness? One reason is because it is the only way to deal with our guilt. Down inside we feel unclean and ashamed for what we've done—but when we turn to Christ and seek His forgiveness, that burden of guilt is lifted.

Do not be deceived.... A man reaps what he sows.
GALATIANS 6:7

MAY 7

In the Bible, God calls us to work for peace and pray for peace.
But He also warns us that conflicts and wars will always be part
of human society until Jesus comes at the end of history to set up
His Kingdom of peace and justice. In that day all evil will be
eliminated, and perfect peace will reign upon the earth.
Until that day, however, the world will always be subject to
"wars and rumors of wars" (Matthew 24:6).

But even when wars rage, we can have peace in our heart
as we open our life to Christ. Ask God to give you that peace
—and pray that others will know it too.

War will continue until the end.
DANIEL 9:26

AUGUST 24

Our tongues have enormous power—both for good and for evil.
The apostle James put it this way: "The tongue also is a fire, a world
of evil among the parts of the body.... With the tongue we praise
our Lord and Father, and with it we curse men, who have been made
in God's likeness" (James 3:6, 9).

Commit your tongue to God. Beyond that, commit your whole
inner being to Christ, and ask Him to cleanse you of anger and hate,
and fill you instead with His love and patience.

A gentle answer turns away wrath, but a harsh word stirs up anger.
PROVERBS 15:1

MAY 8

I've learned that serving the Lord requires prayer, and often means tears....

Power for life, for ministry, doesn't come from our own ability; it comes from God. We need a fresh, daily anointing from the Holy Spirit, and that comes from the time we spend with God in His Word and in prayer.

John Vassar knocked on the door of a person's home and asked the woman if she knew Christ as her Savior. She replied, "It's none of your business" and slammed the door in his face. He stood on the doorstep and wept and wept, and she looked out her window and saw him weeping. The next Sunday she was in church. She said it was because of those tears.

Dear friends, let us love one another, for love comes from God.
1 JOHN 4:7

AUGUST 23

Many Christians lack assurance of their salvation.
The key is to understand that Christ took away all our sins—not part
of them, but all of them. No matter how good we are we can't save
ourselves—because God's standard is perfection. But Christ—who was
without sin—did for us what we could never do for ourselves: He took
all our sins upon Himself, and He took the death and Hell we deserve.
Depend solely on Christ for your salvation. He paid the price
—and now you owe nothing!

My Father, who has given them to me, is greater than all;
no one can snatch them out of my Father's hand.

JOHN 10:29

MAY 9

Every day the young president of an East Coast company instructed his secretary not to disturb him, because he had an important appointment.

One morning the chairman of the board arrived unannounced and said, "I want to see Mr. Jones."

The secretary answered, "I'm sorry. He cannot be disturbed." The chairman became angry and banged open the door. Upon seeing the president of the corporation on his knees in prayer, the chairman quietly backed out of the office and softly closed the door. He asked the secretary, "Is that usual?"

When she answered, "Yes, sir. Every morning," the chairman replied, "No wonder we come to him for advice."

If any of you lacks wisdom, he should ask God, who gives generously to all without finding fault, and it will be given to him.

JAMES 1:5

AUGUST 22

Often those who seem to be the strongest on the
outside are often the weakest on the inside.

But God sees our weaknesses, and He sees the weaknesses in others
as well. And just as He wants to help us deal with our own weaknesses,
so He wants to use us to help others deal with theirs. Ask God to make
you sensitive to those around you who are weak—whatever their
weakness may be—and to help them, both in practical ways and by
pointing them to Christ and His transforming power and love.

Blessed is he who has regard for the weak.

PSALM 41:1

MAY 10

Cover to cover, the Bible tells of people whose prayers were answered and who turned the tide of history as a result. Hezekiah prayed, and God spared his nation when the Assyrians attacked. Elijah prayed, and God sent fire to confound the false prophets and consume the offering on the waterlogged altar. Elisha prayed, and the son of the Shunammite woman was raised from the dead. Jesus prayed, and Lazarus came forth from the tomb. Paul prayed, and new churches were born. The early church prayed, and Peter was delivered from prison.

We can change the course of events if we go to our knees in believing prayer.

[Hezekiah prayed,] "O Lord our God, deliver us from [the enemy's] hand, so that all kingdoms on earth may know that you alone, O Lord, are God." That night the angel of the Lord went out and put to death a hundred and eighty-five thousand men in the Assyrian camp.

2 KINGS 19:19, 35

When we have problems, they have a way of blocking out
everything (and everyone) else. And it's not necessarily wrong to
give attention to our own problems and—with God's help—to overcome
them if we can. But when our problems deafen us to the hurts of
others...when they make us fail to reach out to someone we could help...
then we have become part of the darkness instead of shining like
stars and holding out the word of life as we should.

*[Be] blameless and pure, children of God without fault
in a crooked and depraved generation, in which you shine
like stars in the universe as you hold out the word of life.*

PHILIPPIANS 2:15–16

MAY 11

Whenever we pray, we need to remember that God's
ways and God's timing aren't always the same as ours.
In fact, His time frame rarely matches ours.

We also need to remember that God is able to do what we can't do.
Only He can convict nonbelievers of their sins; only He can convince
them of the truth of the Gospel. That is why no one is hopeless,
for God can break through even the hardest heart. "Is not my word...
like a hammer that breaks a rock in pieces?" (Jeremiah 23:29).

Will not God bring about justice for his chosen ones,
who cry out to him day and night?

LUKE 18:7

AUGUST 20

The most common charge leveled against the Christian faith
is that Christians are "just a bunch of hypocrites."

Sadly, those who make such a charge often have someone in
mind who claimed to be a Christian, but didn't act like it.

What they may not know, however, is that some of Jesus' strongest
words were reserved for hypocrites—for people who claimed to believe
in God and follow His laws, but in reality lived only for themselves.
He compared them to "whitewashed tombs, which look beautiful
on the outside but inside are full of dead men's bones and
everything unclean" (Matthew 23:27).

If you love me, you will obey what I command.

JOHN 14:15

MAY 12

I remember hearing a professor say that during His earthly ministry Jesus probably repeated Himself more than five hundred times.

In college I had a professor who deliberately repeated himself three times. He said that the people in the first two or three rows will get the message the first time. The second time the people in the middle of the lecture hall will get it. The third time the people in the back will get it. And the ones in the front row will never forget it.

We need to keep that fact of human nature in mind as we share God's love with the people He puts in our path.

[My word] will not return to me empty, but will accomplish what I desire and achieve the purpose for which I sent it.

ISAIAH 55:11

AUGUST 19

Jesus Himself claimed He was divine. "I and the Father are one," he stated (John 10:30). His miracles backed up His claim, as did His assertion that He could forgive sins—something only God can do (see Luke 5:20–25).

In addition, repeatedly the Gospel writers pointed out the way He fulfilled the Old Testament's prophecies concerning the Messiah, who was to be called "Immanuel—which means, 'God with us'" (Matthew 1:23). But Jesus' divinity was demonstrated most of all by His resurrection from the dead and His ascension into Heaven—events that were witnessed by hundreds.

The gospel he promised beforehand through his prophets in the Holy Scriptures regarding his Son...who through the Spirit of holiness was declared with power to be the Son of God by his resurrection from the dead: Jesus Christ our Lord.

ROMANS 1:2-4

MAY 13

We also need to flee these things that God has labeled wrong. We need
to flee pride—that tendency to think of ourselves more highly than we
ought—and instead live with humility. We need to flee envy and jealousy.
We need to avoid causing strife, and the anger, bad temper, irritability,
and self-centeredness that prompt it. We need to avoid abusive language
and instead develop a Spirit-controlled tongue. We are also to flee lust,
the love of money, and evil thoughts about other people.

And you and I can do all this by the power of God's Spirit.

*Flee from all this, and pursue righteousness, godliness, faith,
love, endurance and gentleness.*

1 TIMOTHY 6:11

AUGUST 18

Have you ever stopped to think about all the things you accept by faith every day? By faith we assume the pharmacist filled the prescription correctly. By faith you assumed that when you put your feet on the floor this morning it wouldn't collapse. Faith is a much greater part of life than most of us realize.

A skeptic may protest that these are things we can see and touch, whereas God is not. But look at the world around you, with all of its beauty and complexity. Isn't it more logical to believe that behind it is an all-powerful and all-wise Creator, than to think it happened by chance?

This righteousness from God comes through
faith in Jesus Christ to all who believe.
ROMANS 3:22

MAY 14

One night in 1949 I knelt before a stump in the woods of Forest Home, California, opened my Bible and said, "O God, there are many things in this Book I do not understand. But by faith I accept it—from Genesis to Revelation—as Your Word." From that moment on I have never had a single doubt that the Bible is God's Word.

This confidence in God's Word...provides a solid foundation for one's life. We who trust in God's Word aren't living according to what someone says about the Bible, or on some human philosophy. We are basing our faith, our ministry, even our life itself on God's unchanging truth as it is presented in His unchanging Word.

All Scripture is God-breathed and is useful for teaching, rebuking, correcting and training in righteousness.

2 TIMOTHY 3:16

AUGUST 17

Advertisers know that we're more likely to buy a product if they can convince us that everyone else uses it. "If everyone else is using it, then it must be good, and I ought to buy it"—or so they hope we'll say to ourselves.

Jesus calls us to take another path—His path. Yes, it may be harder, and far fewer take it. But it alone offers us true peace and joy—the kind that can only come from knowing God. And it alone leads to eternal life and Heaven. On which path are you? Don't let another day go by without Christ.

Wide is the gate and broad is the road that leads to destruction, and many enter through it.

MATTHEW 7:13

MAY 15

I was preaching in Africa to a small group of tribal people.
They had heard very little about the gospel, and I wanted to bring a
basic, straightforward gospel message they could understand.
So I preached on John 3:16 as simply as I knew how. Trying to explain
John 3:16, I used every illustration I could think of that would help
make the message clear. Afterward—by the work of the Spirit
—several people indicated that they wanted to receive Christ.

Human hearts are the same the world over—in rebellion against God,
suffering from the disease of sin, and dying...until they discover the
simple (and yet profound) truth of God's love for us in Jesus Christ.

*For God so loved the world that he gave his one and only Son,
that whoever believes in him shall not perish but have eternal life.*

JOHN 3:16

AUGUST 16

The Bible says we weren't meant to be alone. Even in the Garden of Eden—long before sin entered the world—God knew that Adam needed someone with whom he could share his life, and so He created Eve. When loneliness afflicts you, remember two truths. First, we are never alone when we know Christ. You can't see Him—but He is more real than the chair you are sitting in, and He is with you.

Second, learn to reach out to others. All around you are people who are lonely. Ask God to help you be a friend to someone who is going through hard times.

The Lord God said, "It is not good for the man to be alone."
GENESIS 2:18

MAY 16

The human mind—like nature itself—abhors a vacuum.
If our minds and hearts are not filled with God's truth,
something else will take His place: cynicism, occultism,
false religions and philosophies, drugs—the list is endless.

Already a terrifying spiritual and moral tide of evil has
loosed our society from its spiritual moorings. Ideas that could
easily destroy our freedoms are rushing into the vacuum that
results when societies turn from the moral truths found in Scripture.

May we who know God's truth stay committed to the principles
outlined in His Word. Above all, may we be salt and light in this world,
proclaiming God's righteousness and love to a confused and dying world.

You are the salt of the earth.... You are the light of the world.

MATTHEW 5:13-14

AUGUST 15

Why is it easier to see someone else's faults than to see our own?
I can think of several reasons—but one of the strongest is because
we naturally love ourselves more than we love other people. And because
we love ourselves, we don't like to criticize ourselves or admit our faults—
because that can be painful, and we don't like pain.

But the Bible tells us to love others just as much as we love ourselves.
Jesus, in fact, taught that this commandment—along with the
commandment to love God above all else—summarizes
God's Law (see Luke 10:27).

Love your neighbor as yourself.
LEVITICUS **19:18**

MAY 17

Blind Bartimaeus probably never expected to be able to see
—and then Jesus Christ came to town.

When He did, Bartimaeus cried out, and he cried out for
the right thing: he cried for mercy. He needed other things, but what
he—like you and I—needed most of all was God's mercy.
Bartimaeus also cried out to the right Person. He cried to the
Lord Jesus Christ, the only One in all the world who could help him.

Third, Bartimaeus cried out at the right time. The Bible says, "Now is the
time of God's favor, now is the day of salvation" (2 Cor. 6:2).

*When [blind Bartimaeus] heard that it was Jesus of Nazareth,
he began to shout, "Jesus, Son of David, have mercy on me!"*

MARK 10:47

AUGUST 14

Look again at that first sentence in the Bible: "In the beginning God created the heavens and the earth." Can you even begin to comprehend the power it took to bring into being the billions of stars that astronomers are still discovering with their telescopes?

Can you even begin to comprehend the wisdom it took to develop the complex laws that would govern the whole creation and give it order—from the smallest subatomic particle to the swirling galaxies of outer space?

Don't ever underestimate God's power—and don't ever underestimate His love. And because of His power and love, He is worthy of our trust and our worship.

In the beginning God created the heavens and the earth.

GENESIS 1:1

MAY 18

The Holy Spirit comes to convict us of our sin. He makes us admit to ourselves that we are sinners. We cannot come to Christ unless the Holy Spirit convicts us of our sin. He also convinces us of the truth about Christ as the Savior.

In addition, the Holy Spirit gives us new life. When we give our lives to Jesus and trust Him as our Savior and Lord, the Spirit renews our souls and brings the life of God into us. We have joy and peace, and we have a new direction to our lives because the Spirit of God has imparted to us the very life of God.

When [the Holy Spirit] has come, He will convict the world of sin, and of righteousness, and of judgment.

JOHN 16:8 NKJV

AUGUST 13

I suppose I've been asked it almost more than any other question over the years: What is the unforgivable sin? Very often the person who is asking is convinced they have committed it.

But notice what Jesus first said: "All the sins and blasphemies of men will be forgiven them."

There is only one exception: the person who deliberately rejects the Holy Spirit's witness that Jesus is the Savior, sent from Heaven to save us from our sins. The only sin God cannot forgive is the sin of rejecting Christ. Turn to Him in repentance and faith—and He will forgive.

I tell you the truth, all the sins and blasphemies of men will be forgiven them. But whoever blasphemes against the Holy Spirit will never be forgiven; he is guilty of an eternal sin.

MARK 3:28–29

MAY 19

There are three reasons why people don't
want to believe in the return of Christ.

First, they claim that Jesus' return did not take
place as the early church hoped—so it must be a myth.

Second, the theory of inevitable progress keeps some people
from believing that Jesus is coming back. Why do we need
Christ to come back if we can reach perfection on our own?

Third, the teaching of Christ's return cuts across the plans and dreams of
millions of people. They want to eat, drink, and be merry and have their
pleasures endlessly. Christ's return would interrupt what they are doing.

But Jesus will return despite these denials.

I will come back and take you to be with me.

JOHN 14:3

AUGUST 12

Instead of giving God His rightful place at the center of our lives, we have substituted the "god" of Self. Only Christ can change our hearts—and through us begin to change our world.

Does this mean we can never make any progress against the massive problems that assail us—poverty, war, injustice, famine, sickness, disease? No, of course not; God wants us to fight evil wherever it is found. But our greatest need is for repentance and spiritual renewal.

Pray that this may happen—beginning with you.

For from within, out of men's hearts, come evil thoughts, sexual immorality, theft, murder, adultery, greed, malice, deceit, lewdness, envy, slander, arrogance and folly.

MARK 7:21–22

MAY 20

First, the sobering news.

When Jesus returns, there will be an accounting given,
a judgment held. Every person outside of Christ will give an
account not only of the things done and the things said,
but also an account of all their thoughts and motives.

Now for the glorious news: When Jesus returns, all evil will
be destroyed. There will be worldwide justice, and complete
safety and security. There will be no more war, no more fighting
—for Jesus Christ will rule as King of kings and Lord of lords,
and "his kingdom will never end" (Luke 1:33).

*They will beat their swords into plowshares and their
spears into pruning hooks. Nation will not take up sword
against nation, nor will they train for war anymore.*

MICAH 4:3

AUGUST 11

The apostle Paul knew what it meant to be persecuted; even a quick survey of Acts reveals that he and his companions encountered opposition almost everywhere they went. Millions of Christians experience the same reality every day.

You may never meet them this side of eternity—but their commitment and courage should challenge and inspire us all.

We may not face the same situation they do—but every believer knows what it is to swim against the stream of an unbelieving world. The friend or relative who mocks you... the business associate who scorns your integrity... the indifference of those around you to moral and spiritual values. But don't let them sway you.

Everyone who wants to live a godly life in
Christ Jesus will be persecuted.

2 TIMOTHY 3:12

MAY 21

Astronomers tell us that every star moves with precision along its celestial path. To ignore the detailed rules of the universe would spell ruin to a star. The laws of nature are fixed, and for a star to ignore those laws would be folly—if it were even possible.

If the laws in His material realm are so fixed and exact, would God be haphazard in the spiritual realm, where the eternal destinies of billions of people are at stake? No! Just as God has equations and rules in the material realm, He also has equations and rules in the spiritual realm.

It is by grace you have been saved, through faith
—and this not from yourselves, it is the gift of God.

EPHESIANS 2:8

AUGUST 10

"Live for yourself," the world proclaims. But God calls us to another way—His way. Blessing, He says, comes only from following Him. Every other way promises what it cannot deliver—and delivers exactly the opposite of what it promised. Some of the most miserable people I have ever known were highly successful in the eyes of the world. But down inside they were restless and spiritually empty.

Have you fallen into the world's trap, following its self-indulgent goals and driven by its self-centered motives? Make sure Christ is first in your life, and make it your goal to live according to His Word.

Blessed are they whose ways are blameless,
who walk according to the law of the Lord.

PSALM 119:1

MAY 22

The Bible says that in Heaven there are two sets of books.
One set records every detail of our lives: everything we have done since
the day we were born. All of that will be held against us at judgment.
But Scripture tells us there is another book in Heaven: the Book of Life.
When we come to Christ...when we believe that He is risen and we
receive Him into our lives—our names are blotted out of the first set
of books. God no longer even remembers our sins because they have
been blotted out by the blood of Christ, shed on the cross for us.

If anyone's name was not found written in the
book of life, he was thrown into the lake of fire.

REVELATION 20:15

AUGUST 9

Is the world getting worse? Is the devil working
more furiously today than ever before?

To many observers this certainly seems to be the case. Take the
record of the last century: two world wars and other conflicts
that killed more people than all previous wars combined; six million
Jews mercilessly killed in the Holocaust;...more Christians martyred
for their faith than at any other time in history.

Why will it be like this? The reason, the Bible says, is because
Satan will lash out in one final burst of fury, seeking with all his
might to block Christ's victory.

*But mark this: There will be terrible times in the last days...evil men
and imposters will go from bad to worse, deceiving and being deceived.*
2 TIMOTHY 3:1, 13

MAY 23

What is your fear? Do you fear the future? Do you fear
life's burdens that sometimes seem almost overwhelming?
Do you fear death? Most of us fear everything except God
—yet it is God whom we should fear most of all!

Jesus can put an end to fear for all who trust in Him.
He is the answer to any fear you have. After all, God's power
is greater than the powers of evil, and "neither death nor life,
neither angels nor demons, neither the present nor the future...
nor anything else in all creation, will be able to separate us from the
love of God that is in Christ Jesus our Lord" (Romans 8:38–39).

There is no fear in love. But perfect love drives out fear.

1 JOHN 4:18

AUGUST 8

Is everything that happens to us already determined by God?
Or do we have the ability to carry out plans on our own,
regardless of what God hoped would happen?

Theologians have disagreed about this for centuries—some stressing God's
absolute control over everything, others emphasizing our freedom to act on
our own. And the reason they haven't agreed is because the Bible teaches
both God's sovereignty and our human responsibility. To us this sounds like
a contradiction—and one I don't believe we'll fully understand until we get
to Heaven. Until that day, we need to hold firmly to both truths: God is in
control of everything, but we also are responsible for our actions.

It is God who works in you to will and to
act according to his good purpose.

PHILIPPIANS 2:13

MAY 24

You'll never be good enough to go to Heaven.
Does that mean there is no hope? No ! Because of Jesus,
you and I have hope. God loves us and wants us to be with Him in
Heaven forever. To make that possible, He sent Christ into the world.
Jesus, who was God in human flesh, was without sin—but on the cross
all our sins were transferred to Him and He died in our place.
We deserve to die for our sins, but Christ took our death and our Hell.
Now we can be forgiven! Now we can enter Heaven!

*God made him who had no sin to be sin for us,
so that in him we might become the righteousness of God.*

2 CORINTHIANS 5:21

AUGUST 7

There is much about Heaven we don't know; God hasn't chosen to reveal everything to us. But we do know Heaven will be far more glorious than anything we can imagine.

One truth God has revealed to us, however, is one we sometimes overlook: In Heaven we will have new bodies—bodies that will be free from the pain and death of this present world. They will be like Christ's body after His resurrection—somewhat like our present bodies, yet free from the limitations we now experience.

Though the doors were locked, Jesus came and stood among them.
JOHN 20:26

MAY 25

God gave us the book of Revelation to encourage us and show us there is hope for the future—and the reason is because the future is in His hands.

Look at it this way: How would you feel if you only read the daily headlines? You'd probably conclude that the world is caught in a never-ending cycle of war, crime, and violence; it would be easy to become cynical and discouraged.

But Revelation gives us a different picture. Someday, it says, Jesus will triumph over all the forces of death and Hell and Satan. All evil and death will be destroyed, and His victory over sin and Satan will be complete.

Blessed is the one who reads the words of this prophecy, and blessed are those who hear it and take to heart what is written in it, because the time is near.

REVELATION 1:3

AUGUST 6

When you face a decision about your future, seek God's will above all else. Make your decision a matter of prayer, and ask Him to guide. If we are truly open to His will, He will direct us.

Does this mean we should just wait around until God gives us some kind of miraculous sign or deep inner conviction? No, not necessarily. God wants us to be practical. Do research if you need to; understand yourself and your gifts; seek the advice of others. Make your decision in the light of God's Word also; God never leads us to do anything that is contrary to the Bible.

In all your ways acknowledge [God],
and he will make your paths straight.
PROVERBS 3:6

MAY 26

Do people who have died and gone to Heaven know what happens on earth? The Bible doesn't give us an absolutely clear answer about this, but it does hint that they may be aware of what takes place here on earth.

[In Hebrews 11] the writer paints a picture for us—a picture of a stadium filled with spectators, perhaps watching us as we live out our life and cheering us on as we stretch toward the finish line. What we do know for sure is that God sees us—and that should be enough to encourage us to live for Christ and do what is right.

Nothing in all creation is hidden from God's sight.

HEBREWS 4:13

AUGUST 5

Young children can ask the most amazing questions about God and Heaven! And when they do, we shouldn't ignore them or act like their questions aren't important—because they are.

When children ask you about God, do your best to answer simply and honestly in terms they can understand. Of course they don't need deep and complicated answers, but just because they can't understand everything about God doesn't mean they can't understand something about Him. I don't understand electricity, but that doesn't mean I can't turn on a light switch.

Let the little children come to me, and do not hinder them, for the kingdom of God belongs to such as these.

MARK 10:14

MAY 27

I have to admit that I do not know why some people suffer more than others do. This world is not the way God meant it to be; it is in the grip of "spiritual forces of evil in the heavenly realms" (Ephesians 6:12).

In light of that truth, we must not blame God for everything that happens in our life, especially the bad things. Instead, we need to remember that God has already entered the battle against evil—and some day His victory will be complete. In His death and resurrection, Jesus Christ confronted Satan—and won! That is our hope—and that is our comfort.

In this world you will have trouble.
But take heart! I have overcome the world!
JOHN 16:33

AUGUST 4

Why doesn't [Satan] just give up and stop bothering us?
Perhaps he still expects to win. After all, Satan totally rejects everything
about God—including His promises. But Satan also persists because he
has one main goal: to block God's work in any way he can. As long as he
is active, people will be deceived into following his way instead of God's
way. Even believers can be diverted from God's plan for their life and be
content with a lukewarm faith that makes little impact on others.

Yes, some day Satan will be defeated.

*Thrown into the lake of burning sulfur...[and] tormented day
and night for ever and ever.*

REVELATION 20:10

MAY 28

God's standard is nothing less than perfection. That means we can't make it into Heaven on our own, for no matter how good we are, we still aren't perfect. Even the best person sins in words and actions, as well as in thoughts and motives. God's standard is perfection and even one sin will keep us out of Heaven.

So if you know someone who thinks good deeds are their ticket to Heaven, urge them not to gamble with their soul. Instead, urge them to repent of their pride and trust Jesus alone for their salvation.

There is no one righteous, not even one.

ROMANS 3:10

AUGUST 3

Has it ever bothered you that some people who turn their backs on God seem to go through life without ever having anything bad happen to them?

We don't know their hearts. We also need to remember that God sees the whole picture, while we see only a little part. God knows what He is doing, and He can be trusted to do what is right according to His perfect plan. Sadly, these people will one day die and face God. God's goodness to them should have caused them to turn to Him in thankfulness and trust—but instead they ignored His blessings and lived only for themselves. How tragic to enter eternity unprepared.

Do you show contempt for the riches of his kindness, tolerance and patience, not realizing that God's kindness leads you toward repentance?

ROMANS 2:4

MAY 29

I find it very encouraging that God included real-life, flesh-and-blood sinful people in His Word. David committed adultery, Abraham lied about his wife—the list goes on and on. Why are they in the Bible? So we will learn from their wrongdoings.

One lesson is that sin always has consequences. God has much to teach us from the examples of His people who failed. But most of all His Word points us to Christ, who alone can forgive us and set our feet on the right path.

These things happened to them as examples and were written down as warnings for us.

1 CORINTHIANS 10:11

AUGUST 2

The only thing that counts as far as our salvation is concerned is our relationship to Jesus Christ. If you have acknowledged your sinfulness and truly trusted Christ to save you, then nothing can take away your salvation.

If we are committed to Jesus, however, God also wants us to become part of a fellowship of believers. God wants us to grow in our faith, and one of the ways we do this is through our fellowship with other believers. Ask God to lead you to a church—to a body of believers—where you can grow spiritually.

For we are members of [Christ's] body.

Ephesians 5:30

MAY 30

You can seldom argue a person into the kingdom of God. That's because the real reason for disbelief in God usually has nothing to do with logic. [It] has to do with their emotions and their will. In other words, people don't believe in God because they don't want to believe—and they don't want to believe because they want to run their own lives.

We must do our best to answer—with gentleness and respect —any question we're asked, even if we think it isn't sincere or is only meant to put us on the spot. But the most important thing we can do is to show by our life and love that Jesus is real.

Let your conversation be always full of grace, seasoned with salt, so that you may know how to answer everyone.

COLOSSIANS 4:6

AUGUST 1

If you could know beyond a shadow of a doubt that God had completely forgiven you, what reason would you have to keep feeling guilty? Absolutely none.

And God offers you exactly that: complete and total forgiveness, no matter what you have done. Jesus willingly took your sins and mine upon Himself, and He paid the penalty we deserved. We don't need to wonder if we've been forgiven; we don't need to carry around a burden of guilt.

As far as the east is from the west, so far has he removed our transgressions from us.

PSALM 103:12

MAY 31

Within fifty days of Jesus' death and the apparent collapse of His cause, the city of Jerusalem rang with the cries of those who boldly declared that God had raised Jesus from the dead, and that they were eyewitnesses to that truth. Hundreds had seen the resurrected Jesus!

As the Holy Spirit descended on the day of Pentecost, craven cowards were changed into courageous confessors. Humble fishermen became heralds of the King. All who saw and heard them were compelled to acknowledge that something had utterly transformed their lives. When questioned by their critics, the apostles did not hesitate to reply: they accounted for their boldness by pointing to the risen Christ.

They saw what seemed to be tongues of fire....
All of them were filled with the Holy Spirit.

ACTS 2:3–4

JULY 31

Some day we each will die and stand before God to give an account of our lives—and if we have ignored God and turned away from His offer of salvation, we can only expect His judgment. The Bible is clear: "Man is destined to die once, and after that to face judgment" (Hebrews 9:27).

Those are sobering words that we ignore at our peril.

But the Bible warns us that God also brings judgment upon us in this life. The Bible says, "You may be sure that your sin will find you out" (Numbers 32:23).

For it is time for judgment to begin with the family of God, and if it begins with us, what will the outcome be for those who do not obey the gospel of God?

1 PETER 4:17

JUNE 1

What are you afraid of?

Our emotions can lie to us, and we need to counter our emotions with truth.

And the greatest truth you can use to counteract your fears is the truth that God loves you and His plans for you are good. So give your fears—and every aspect of your life—to Christ. Then let the truth of His Word, the Bible, take root in your soul every day, and trust your future to Him who knows your needs and loves you deeply.

I know the plans I have for you...plans to prosper you and not to harm you, plans to give you hope and a future.

JEREMIAH 29:11

JULY 30

The Bible's message is centered in Jesus Christ, God's one and only Son—who He is and what He has done for us by His death and resurrection. When we read its pages, we discover that Jesus was not only a great man, but He was God in human flesh, "the exact representation of [God's] being."

Why is this important? Because only a divine Savior can save us from our sins. We cannot save ourselves; even one sin, the Bible teaches, would be enough to keep us out of Heaven.

The Son is the radiance of God's glory and
the exact representation of his being.

HEBREWS 1:3

JUNE 2

Have you ever known someone who had lots of questions about God and the Bible? No matter how many you answered, they always had more!

Our faith can stand up to any question, but sometimes people ask questions—and keep asking questions—just to avoid facing their own spiritual needs and acknowledging who Jesus really is. Their questions may only be an excuse to keep from turning their life over to Christ. Make sure your friend knows what the gospel is; many people really don't understand it—although they think they do. Never give up hoping that someday they will give their life to Jesus.

And of course pray for them; only God can change hearts.

Take my yoke upon you and learn from me.
MATTHEW 11:29

JULY 29

The way we live often speaks far louder than our words. People may tell us they don't believe the Bible—but they can't deny its power as they see it change our life, guide our decisions, and influence how we live. Ask God to rule in your heart, and remake you from within into the person He wants you to be. Then ask Him to help you be sensitive to those around you who may be successful on the outside, but inwardly are empty and confused, so that by your life and by your words they may discover the joy and peace that come from knowing Christ.

I urge you to live a life worthy of the calling you have received.
EPHESIANS 4:1

JUNE 3

The Old Testament was the Bible Jesus knew and often quoted.
One reason the Old Testament is so important, He declared,
is because it points to His coming as the promised Messiah.

Some parts of the Old Testament may seem hard to understand,
such as the detailed instructions that governed the Old Testament
sacrificial system. These no longer strictly apply to us, however,
because they have been fulfilled in Christ's sacrifice of Himself on
the cross—and yet they still have much to teach us about the holiness of
God and the seriousness of sin—profound truths we need to understand.

*Man does not live on bread alone but on every word that
comes from the mouth of the Lord.*

DEUTERONOMY 8:3

JULY 28

If God wants you to serve in this position, He will make it clear to you. Once you accept the invitation to serve, know that as you turn to God and rely on Him, He will empower and guide you. Do all you need to do to be ready to serve in whatever capacity God calls you, and realize that the knowledge of God's Word is an essential tool for any aspect of kingdom work.

Don't be afraid to take a step of faith, to respond to God's call to serve.

[God] said to [Paul], "My grace is sufficient for you,
for my power is made perfect in weakness."
2 CORINTHIANS 12:9

JUNE 4

Have you ever been falsely accused of something?
Anger and bitterness—whatever the cause—only end up hurting us.
So, whenever a situation causes you to be angry, turn that anger over
to Christ. Ask Him to forgive your anger, and then ask Him to help
you get rid of it and even forgive the person who hurt you.

Remember that Jesus was falsely accused of sin. Rather than strike
back at His accusers, He willingly went to the cross so that we could
be forgiven for all our sins—including anger.

The tongue also is a fire, a world of evil among the parts of the body.
JAMES 3:6

JULY 27

By His death and resurrection Jesus bridged the gap between
us and God—a gap caused by sin. But simply believing intellectually
that He has done this is not enough. Like that bridge across
the gorge, we must trust Him and commit our lives to Him.
And when we do, we will discover that He can be trusted to save us,
because He truly is the bridge between us and God.

Have you committed your life in faith and trust to
Jesus Christ as your "bridge" and your Savior?

*Salvation is found in no one else, for there is no other name
under heaven given to men by which we must be saved.*

ACTS 4:12

JUNE 5

Paul's preaching in Athens' main marketplace attracted great curiosity, and finally a well-known group of intellectuals invited him to speak to them. He readily accepted, and in his address covered three important points.

First, Paul talked about the one true God, the Creator who is the holy, unchangeable God of love. Calling their attention to an altar he had seen dedicated "To an Unknown God," he pointed them to the God who made them and sustained them. How many people believe God exists but find Him unknown, in the sense that they have no fellowship with Him?

May we know what this new teaching is that you are presenting?
ACTS 17:19

J U L Y 2 6

A church should be a place of warmth and fellowship, and a place where even the newest member or latest visitor feels welcome and at home. Is this true in your church? Simply attending a worship service doesn't automatically mean closer relationships with others.

If you are an "old-timer" in your church, go out of your way to welcome visitors and new members. And if you are a visitor or new member, make a special effort to get to know people. Find out what activities the church offers for spiritual growth.

[You are] fellow citizens with God's people and members of God's household.

EPHESIANS 2:19

JUNE 6

An eight-year-old asked me the other day,
"How old is God?" I told him he'd asked a very good question
and said I was glad he wanted to know more about God.

Then I told this young child that God is timeless: He has
always existed. God has no beginning—and He has no end.
He was never young, and He will never grow old.

Why is this important? Because this means you can
trust God with your life. He won't die or grow weak or forgetful;
He loves you, and He is always there to take care of you.
That's an important truth, whatever our age!

*Before the mountains were born or you brought forth the
earth and the world, from everlasting to everlasting you are God.*

PSALM 90:2

JULY 25

God's will is for us to live at peace with everyone—but sometimes
the door to a broken relationship seems closed forever.

If someone rejects us and absolutely refuses to have anything to do with
us, we can't force them to change. But we can—and should—do everything
we can to keep the door open to a possible reconciliation. We shouldn't strike
back or condemn; instead, we should let them know we still care, and that
we hope someday his or her attitude will change. And if we were at
fault—even in small ways—we need to admit it and ask for forgiveness.

If it is possible, as far as it depends on you,
live at peace with everyone.

ROMANS 12:18

JUNE 7

Grace means "undeserved favor or goodness." God doesn't owe us anything—yet in His grace, He still gives us good things. We don't even deserve the next breath we take, but God in His grace grants it. Most of all, we don't deserve to go to Heaven, but in His grace God has provided the way: He sent Jesus Christ to die for our sins.

We are sinners, and sin is rebellion against God. We don't like to admit this. We like to think we aren't so bad after all, and God ought to overlook our sins. But that's just not true.

Thank God for His saving grace.

Your eyes are too pure to look on evil; you cannot tolerate wrong.
HABAKKUK 1:13

JULY 24

It is not a sin to long for Heaven. If we know Jesus, we know that in Heaven all our burdens and pain will be lifted forever. It is, as the apostle Paul stated, "better by far" to be in Heaven with Jesus than to be suffering on this sin-filled earth. At the same time, though, God has a purpose in keeping us here until He finally takes us home. He has things to teach us about Himself, and He can still use us to bless others.

Keep your eyes on eternity—but also seek Christ's will for you right now, no matter what you are facing.

I desire to depart and be with Christ, which is better by far.

PHILIPPIANS 1:23

JUNE 8

I believe only God knows the future and that we are to look to Him —not to the stars or the tea leaves or the lines on the palm of our hand—for our confidence in the future. Some of these attempts to learn what the future holds are merely foolish or useless, but others involve occult practices that can bring people into contact with spiritual forces that are not from God, but from Satan.

This is one reason why the Bible strongly urges us to avoid any practice that may be linked with the occult.

Trust in God; trust also in me...I am going there to prepare a place for you.

JOHN 14:1–2

JULY 23

Are there some things God cannot do? The answer may
surprise you: Yes, there are some things that God can't do.
God cannot, for instance, tell a lie or go back on His promises.
Neither can He do something evil or have an impure thought. Why?
Because God cannot do anything that is contrary to His basic character.

Not only is He perfect, but He is also absolutely sovereign and
all-powerful. And because of that—as Jeremiah wrote—nothing
is too hard for Him. If He could bring Jesus back from the dead,
can't He also help you overcome whatever situation you are facing today?

*Sovereign Lord, you have made the heavens and the earth
by your great power.... Nothing is too hard for you.*
JEREMIAH 32:17

JUNE 9

Evil is real, and at one time or another most of us have wondered why God doesn't just reach down and stop it. Sometimes He does—but not always, and the Bible says evil is a mystery that we won't fully understand until we get to Heaven. In the meantime, God calls us to trust Him and have confidence in His love, no matter the circumstances. Let your attitude be that of the Psalmist: "But as for me, it is good to be near God. I have made the Sovereign Lord my refuge" (Psalm 73:28). Ask God to help you trust Him even when the way is dark.

I do believe; help me overcome my unbelief!

MARK 9:24

JULY 22

God wants to use you right where you are. Every day you probably come in contact with people who will never enter a church, or talk with a pastor, or open a Bible—and God wants to use you to point them to Christ. You may be the "bridge" God would use to bring them to Himself.

Be alert for opportunities to share the Good News of Christ's love with others—even today. Never underestimate what God can do through even your smallest effort to reach out to others in the name of Jesus.

Be very careful to...serve him with all your heart and all your soul.

JOSHUA 22:5

JUNE 10

C. S. Lewis pointed out that there are only four possible conclusions you can reach about Jesus. Either He was a liar, or He was self-deceived, or He was insane—or He was in fact who He claimed to be: the Son of God. Which was He? The only logical conclusion is that Jesus was the Son of God. A liar couldn't have taught the lofty moral principles He did. A self-deceived person couldn't have performed the miracles He did. A lunatic couldn't have held up under pressure the way Jesus did. After closely observing His life every day, His disciples reached their conclusion: "You are the Christ, the Son of the living God" (Matthew 16:16).

Who do you say I am?
MATTHEW 16:15

JULY 21

We have become like the people of Jeremiah's day: "They have no shame at all; they do not even know how to blush" (Jeremiah 8:12). If we are to be pure and holy, we must first commit ourselves—mind, body, and spirit—completely to Christ. We can't hold back any area of our life from Him. Second, we must avoid situations that might encourage impure thoughts or actions. And, third, we must fill our mind and heart with Christ by feeding our souls on a daily diet of prayer and God's Word. With God's help we can keep our way pure, by living according to His Word.

How can a young man keep his way pure? By living according to your word.
PSALM 119:9

JUNE 11

Some of Jesus' strongest words were reserved for hypocrites—for people who claimed to believe in God, yet were insincere and only used their religion to try to impress others. Jesus called those people "whitewashed tombs, which look beautiful on the outside but on the inside are full of dead men's bones" (Matthew 23:27). What an indictment!

Ask God to reveal hypocrisy in your life—an inconsistency between what you profess and what you practice. Then ask God to bring you so close to Christ that you won't have any desire to live an inconsistent, deceitful life.

Rid yourselves of all malice and all deceit,
hypocrisy, envy, and slander of every kind.

1 PETER 2:1

JULY 20

From beginning to end, the Bible proclaims this simple truth: God loves you.

Why, then, hasn't God apparently come into your life? The key word
is apparently. If you have confessed your sin and acknowledged that
Jesus is your Lord, who died on the cross for you and rose again to give
you eternal life, then God has promised to forgive you and save you.
God does not lie, and He has promised that if we truly commit our life
to Christ, He will save us and come into our life. Salvation is God's gift
to you—a gift paid for by Christ's sacrifice of Himself for you.

*If you confess with your mouth, "Jesus is Lord," and believe
in your heart that God raised him from the dead, you will be saved.*

ROMANS 10:9

JUNE 12

Don't be afraid to challenge your non-believing friends to read the Gospels and learn about Jesus for themselves. God can use it to break down their barriers and bring them to Himself.

Also pray for them. You can't change their heart and mind—but God can. Ask Him to awaken your friends to their need for Christ. Finally, be a good witness by the way you live. Let these friends know you really care; let them see Jesus' love and peace and joy in your life. The way we live is often more convincing than the words we say.

But you are a chosen people...that you may declare the praises of him who called you out of darkness into his wonderful light.

1 PETER 2:9

JULY 19

I find it significant that God placed the young Jesus in a family. Did you allow anger and bitterness to poison your relationship with your parents—even over things that happened many years ago? Don't let your parents' failures—real or imagined—hold you in their grip any longer. Instead, ask God to help you forgive the past—and then ask Christ to change you into the person He wants you to be. And if you are a parent, ask God to help you be a loving and wise guide for your children, and to build your family on Christ and His will.

So [Joseph] got up, took the child and his mother and went to the land of Israel...and he went and lived in a town called Nazareth.

MATTHEW 2:21, 23

JUNE 13

Have you ever watched a loved one struggle with pain, growing disability, and even approaching death?

We live in a fallen, sin-scarred world, and much of what happens falls far short of God's original plan.

Even when we can't understand why God allows things like this to happen, He still can be trusted to do what is right. God is sovereign, and He knows what is best—for you, for the person who is suffering, and for all those affected by their suffering. In God's time, He will take the suffering saint to be with Him.

There is a time for everything...a time to be born and a time to die.
ECCLESIASTES 3:1–2

JULY 18

I've found it helpful to counter [worries] with the Bible's promises about God's steadfast love. He loves us and, no matter what happens to us, He never abandons us. We know this because Jesus Christ demonstrated God's love for us by giving His life for our salvation.

Does this mean that things will never go wrong, or we'll never have any problems? Absolutely not! But it does mean that nothing we experience ever catches God by surprise or is too big for Him to handle. Even when our day seems dark, God never leaves us, nor does He allow anything to come our way that can overwhelm us.

From everlasting to everlasting the Lord's love is with those who fear him.

PSALM 103:17

JUNE 14

Forgiveness isn't easy. In fact, often we can't forgive the person who hurt us deeply without God's help. But is it impossible for God to overcome those hurts and heal the wounds? No, of course not.

Remember what it cost Christ to forgive you—and then ask Him to help you forgive others. What the person did was wrong, and you may still bear the emotional scars. But God doesn't want you to carry those hurts forever.

Whom do you need to forgive before it's too late?

Now instead you ought to forgive and comfort him,
so that he will not be overwhelmed by excessive sorrow.

2 CORINTHIANS 2:7

JULY 17

God looks at our finances differently. First, He knows that our giving is a measure of something far more important: The depth of our commitment to Jesus Christ. And it isn't just a question of how much we give, but what our attitude is as we give. Do we give reluctantly or under compulsion (perhaps to impress other people)? If so, it strongly suggests that we love ourselves more than we love Christ. Don't let this be true of you.

But God also is able to take what we give and use it in ways we could never imagine.

Each man should give what he has decided in his heart to give, not reluctantly or under compulsion, for God loves a cheerful giver.
2 CORINTHIANS 9:7

JUNE 15

I'm afraid we have largely lost sight of the holiness and purity of God today. This is one reason why we tolerate sin so easily, and casually dismiss so many sins as minor or insignificant. It is also the reason why we ignore sin in our lives and neglect to repent of it.

We need a new vision of who God is, and who we are as sinners in His sight. No matter how good we think we are, God's judgment still stands: "there is no one who does good, not even one" (Romans 3:12).

To fear the Lord is to hate evil; I hate pride and arrogance,
evil behavior and perverse speech.

PROVERBS 8:13

JULY 16

Suppose the NASA control center in Houston had received word from Apollo 11 that the astronauts were off course, and had replied, "Oh, that's all right. A number of roads lead to the moon. Just keep on the way you are going." You and I know they would have kept going—but they would never have come back.

People today don't like the word narrow, but Jesus clearly said there are two roads to the future for all of us: the way to Hell and destruction is broad, but the way to Heaven is narrow. Which road are you on?

Small is the gate and narrow the road that leads to life, and only a few find it.

MATTHEW 7:14

JUNE 16

Is the antichrist alive today? No one can say for sure.
But the Bible tells us a very important truth: the spirit of antichrist
has often been among us. Satan is always at work to oppose God's work,
and some people deliberately take their stand with Satan, not God.

What does all this mean? It means we must be sure of our own
commitment to Christ. If our lives are not built on Christ's truth,
we can easily be led astray. Don't let this happen to you!

As you have heard that the antichrist is coming,
even now many antichrists have come.
1 JOHN 2:18

JULY 15

Are you walking on a path that you are realizing is not God's best for you? Do even need to make a complete U-turn, but are struggling to find the courage to do so? For example, is it time to end a wrong relationship, or cast off a habit that isn't healthy, or leave behind an undisciplined life that always seems to put God in second place?

Whatever situation has you feeling stuck, know that there is no shortcut or easy way out. You need to make the right decision—firmly and decisively—and then stick with it with God's help.

There is a way that seems right to a man,
but in the end it leads to death.

PROVERBS 16:25

JUNE 17

We may even think that the more civilized or educated we are, the less likely we will be to do something evil. But that isn't necessarily so. Even people who are decent and respectable on the surface may be harboring deep hatred and anger in their hearts.

Only Jesus can cleanse us from the moral and spiritual filth we have allowed to accumulate in our hearts. When we go to Him, God not only forgives us of our sins, but He comes to live within us by His Holy Spirit. God's promise is for all who turn in faith to Christ: "I will give you a new heart" (Ezekiel 36:26).

The hearts of men, moreover, are full of evil and there is madness in their hearts while they live.

ECCLESIASTES 9:3

JULY 14

Sometimes...we don't know why God allows bad things to happen to us. Even then, however, God can use them to teach us and make us into better people. Disappointments and tragedies, for example, can teach us to turn in trust to God for the hope and comfort we need. These experiences can also teach us patience, and make us more sensitive to others who are suffering.

Are you passing through a difficult time today?
Ask God to use it to increase your faith and make you more like Christ.

We also rejoice in our sufferings, because we know that suffering produces perseverance; perseverance, character; and character, hope.

ROMANS 5:3–4

JUNE 18

Ask God to help you be content with the way you are. God made you, and it's wrong for you to think He made a mistake. Some of the most unhappy people I have ever met possessed great beauty or wealth, yet their lives were empty and without meaning. God loves you just as you are!

Focus on what the Bible calls true beauty—the beauty of a godly character, "the unfading beauty of a gentle and quiet spirit, which is of great worth in God's sight" (1 Peter 3:4).

Your beauty should not come from outward adornment.

1 PETER 3:3

JULY 13

We aren't hypocritical just because we don't meet a person's every demand. Would we really be helping them if we met their every demand, no matter how selfish? Instead, we might just be encouraging greater self-centeredness on their part—and that is not God's will. Sometimes love says no, because that is what is best for the other person.

If you can fulfill someone's request, however, do so even if it involves sacrifice on your part. The Bible says, "let us not love with words or tongue but with actions and in truth" (1 John 3:18).

Greater love has no one than this,
that he lay down his life for his friends.

JOHN 15:13

JUNE 19

Has God ever tried to get your attention? Sometimes a narrow escape in a car accident or a false-positive test for cancer or a major surgery can make us realize that we aren't ready to die —and make us wonder if God is trying to get our attention.

Perhaps, for instance, God is trying to tell you that you are on the wrong road. You may have chosen a self-centered, self-indulgent path—but where does it lead?

When we know Christ we have joy and peace, because we know our future is secure—and some day we will be with Him forever.

No man knows when his hour will come:
As fish are caught in a cruel net...
so men are trapped by evil times
that fall unexpectedly upon them.

ECCLESIASTES 9:12

JULY 12

Few things touch my heart more than the news that some of my brothers and sisters in Christ are being persecuted, tortured, and killed for their love of Jesus.

It has been estimated that more Christians have been killed for their faith during the last one hundred years than in all the other centuries combined since the time of Christ. One reason is the great expansion of Christianity in the last few centuries—often into places of great unbelief and hostility. Another reason is the rise of militantly antireligious political systems.

Remember those in prison as if you were their fellow prisoners, and those who are mistreated as if you yourselves were suffering.

HEBREWS 13:3

JUNE 20

It isn't fashionable today to talk about Hell—but the Bible is clear:
God created us with a soul or a spirit that will live forever—and when
we die, we will continue to exist—either in the place the Bible calls
Heaven or in the place it calls Hell.

Hell, the Bible says, is reserved for those who reject God and turn
their back on Him. If you want nothing to do with Him in this life,
then you will have nothing to do with Him in the next life.

And let me be as clear as possible: you don't want to go to Hell.
Hell is a place of absolute loneliness and hopelessness.

*In hell, where he was in torment, he looked up...and called to him,
"Father Abraham, have pity on me...because I am in agony in this fire."*

LUKE 16:23–24

JULY 11

How do we know Heaven even exists? How do we know it isn't just a myth—a product of our imaginations?

First, I am convinced Heaven exists because God has put the hope of Heaven within our hearts. That hope is almost universal, and it is part of every religion. The Bible says that this hope comes from God.

The main reason I know Heaven exists, however, is the death and resurrection of Jesus. When He died on the cross, He erased the only thing that can keep us out of Heaven: our sin. When He rose from the dead, He guaranteed for all time that there is life after death, and that Heaven is real.

[God] has also set eternity in the hearts of men.
ECCLESIASTES 3:11

JUNE 21

God took upon Himself human flesh and became a man—a fact that should stagger our imagination. If we want to know what God is like, we only need to look at Jesus, for He was God in human flesh.

Pray for people you know who are seeking God, that they won't be deceived or led down a path that will only take them away from God. And ask God to use you point them to Jesus' love and truth. Only Christ can meet the deepest hunger of our souls.

No one has ever seen God, but God the One and Only, who is at the Father's side, has made him known.

JOHN 1:18

JULY 10

Have you ever had a weed in your yard that you chopped down and thought was gone—only to have it spring up again? Its roots, you discovered, were still alive, and they might even have spread.

Sinful thoughts can be like that. When we come to Christ, He begins to change our thinking, and new thoughts begin to take root in our mind—thoughts about God's love for us and His will for our life.

Don't be surprised when old ways of thinking crop up—but don't let them linger. When they come, immediately turn to God and ask Him to help you get rid of them—just as you pull weeds out of your garden.

Let the word of Christ dwell in you richly.
COLOSSIANS 3:16

JUNE 22

Suppose you had a deadly form of cancer, and one day you discovered a cure for it. Wouldn't you want other people who had that same disease to know what you had learned? Wouldn't you try to point them to the same discovery you had made? I'm sure you would; it would be monstrous to do otherwise.

The Bible teaches that we all have a spiritual "cancer" —a deadly spiritual disease called sin. Not only does it cripple us right now morally and spiritually, but it will also destroy us in the future and keep us from the blessings God has for us in Heaven.

Now in Christ Jesus you who once were far away have been brought near through the blood of Christ.

EPHESIANS 2:13

JULY 9

I think Isaiah 6 is one of the most unforgettable chapters in the Bible,
for there we find Isaiah's intimate account of his experience with God.
Isaiah comprehended who God is. The ultimate experience of life is knowing
God, and Isaiah came to know God in His righteousness and holiness.
The challenge: We who see God as He is, are to see the world
as He sees it—and then step out in faith to make difference.

*I heard the voice of the Lord saying, "Whom shall I send?
And who will go for us?" And I said, "Here am I. Send me!"*

ISAIAH 6:8–9

JUNE 23

The Bible tells us that God is loving and merciful—and this is absolutely true. That truth, however, makes some people wonder how He could send anyone to Hell.

But do you honestly think God ought to excuse people like Hitler or Stalin, and tell them He doesn't really care that they killed tens of millions of innocent people?

God can't simply ignore evil or pretend it doesn't exist; to do so would be unjust. If someone hates God and chooses to do evil, God should not overlook their lifelong rebellion. The Bible is very clear: "He has set a day when he will judge the world with justice" (Acts 17:31).

The Lord our God is righteous in everything he does.
DANIEL 9:14

JULY 8

Deep in your heart are you totally surrendered and committed to Christ?
Outwardly the Israelites in Joshua's day were followers of God—but in
their hearts they were idolators. Joshua told them that this hypocrisy
could not continue. They were to decide whether they wanted to serve
the true and living God, or serve their idols. It was Israel's day of
decision. They were to go on record—either for God or against Him.
Likewise, we must decide whom we will serve. After all, a Christian
should forsake everything false and turn wholeheartedly to Jesus.

*These people come near to me with their mouth and honor me
with their lips, but their hearts are far from me.*

ISAIAH 29:13

JUNE 24

Are we living in the end times? Will Jesus return soon? The world does seem to be getting worse, and this should remind us that someday Christ will come again to bring an end to this present world. Jesus taught that certain events or signs would point to His coming, and we certainly see many of these today.

So is Christ's coming near? It may well be—although the Bible warns us not to make precise predictions. But we must be alert and ready for His coming by being certain of our commitment to Christ, and approaching every day as if it were our last.

Therefore keep watch because you do not know when the owner of the house will come back— whether in the evening, or at midnight, or when the rooster crows, or at dawn.

MARK 13:35

JULY 7

As far as the unbelieving world's understanding is concerned, Christianity is a gospel of crisis: It boldly proclaims that this world's days are numbered. Every cemetery testifies that our days on this planet are indeed numbered. The Bible teaches that life is only a vapor that appears for a moment and then vanishes (James 4:14).

There is another sense, however, in which the world-system will end: there will be an end of history and the end of a world that has been dominated by evil. Jesus will come again and set up His kingdom of righteousness and social justice, and hatred, greed, jealousy, war, and death will no longer exist.

Multitudes, multitudes in the valley of decision!
For the day of the Lord is near in the valley of decision.

JOEL 3:14

JUNE 25

Most of us are insensitive to the sufferings of others until we experience them ourselves. We become wrapped up in our own circumstances, and overlook the needs of those around us—even members of our own family. But this isn't God's plan. We are to show our love by bearing one another's burdens.

We can't change the past; it may be too late to apologize to someone for our thoughtlessness. But we don't need to carry around a burden of guilt over this. When Jesus died on the cross, He died for every sin you ever committed, including this one. If you confess your sin, He will cleanse you (1 John 1:9).

Carry each other's burdens, and in this way you will fulfill the law of Christ.

GALATIANS 6:2

JULY 6

Love is not the whole of our spiritual life because it is only one of the virtues God wants us to have. If we ignore the other virtues—such as joy, peace, patience, kindness, goodness, gentleness, and self-control (Galatians 5:22–23)—our life will be unbalanced and incomplete.

Why are these virtues so important? One reason is because these virtues were part of Christ's character—and God's will is that we would become more like Christ. In addition, as the apostle Peter said, "If you possess these qualities in increasing measure, they will keep you from being ineffective and unproductive" (2 Peter 1:8).

Add to your faith goodness; and to goodness, knowledge; and to knowledge, self-control; and to self-control, perseverance; and to perseverance, godliness; and to godliness, brotherly kindness; and to brotherly kindness, love.

2 PETER 1:5–7

JUNE 26

When we are hurting, we value the presence of a friend who will just listen. But when someone we know is hurting, we often are tempted to do anything but listen—chattering away and giving unwanted advice to them, instead of letting them share their burden with us.

But remember: Sometimes the best thing we can do is listen quietly when a friend has a problem, letting them share their feelings and assuring them that we care, even if we don't have any answers.

When your friends are hurting, ask God to help you be an encourager and a burden-bearer.

There is a time for everything…
a time to be silent and a time to speak.

ECCLESIASTES 3:1, 7

JULY 5

I will never forget one picture [from a church in Moldavia].
It is of a stairway to Heaven, and pilgrims are going up the ladder.
Below them are devils trying to pull them down into the flames of hell.
At the top of the picture, Jesus is standing, waiting in Heaven for the
faithful, and above the pilgrims are angels helping them along.
That scene shows the great battle between good and evil, between God
and Satan, that rages in the heavens and on this earth.

Today—and every day—put on the full armor of God to fight Satan's attacks.

*For our struggle is not against flesh and blood but against the
rulers, against the authorities, against the powers of this dark world
and against the spiritual forces of evil in the heavenly realms.*

EPHESIANS 6:12

JUNE 27

If you have honestly turned to Jesus and asked Him to forgive you, then you are forgiven—totally and absolutely. When Jesus died on the cross, every sin you ever committed—every one—was placed on Him. He died to pay the penalty for all your sins.

So don't believe your emotions and don't let the memories of the past defeat you. The Bible says, "The blood of Jesus Christ His Son cleanses us from all sin" (1 John 1:7 NKJV). That is God's promise to you—and God cannot lie.

Cleanse me with hyssop, and I will be clean; wash me, and I will be whiter than snow.

PSALM 51:7

JULY 4

Because they couldn't resolve their conflicts, [the delegates of the Constitutional Convention] picked up their hats and coats and started to leave. Suddenly Benjamin Franklin spoke up.

"What a minute, gentlemen," he is reported to have said. "This country was conceived in faith in God. Many of us here believe in prayer. Let us get upon our knees and pray to Almighty God and see whether God shall give to us the answer to our dilemma."

Upon their knees those men went, and out of that prayer meeting came the immortal Constitution of the United States of America.

What dilemma in your nation—or in your life—is compelling you to get down on your knees and seek God's answer?

If my people...pray and seek my face...I will hear from heaven.

2 CHRONICLES 7:14

JUNE 28

It [is never] too late for you to honestly face your sins
and turn to Jesus in repentance and faith.

God loves each one of us, and yet we hurt Him deeply when
we turn our backs on Him. But He loves us despite our sin,
and He stands ready to forgive us. Forgiveness is not something
we deserve; it only comes as a gift of God's grace.

Don't let another day go by without Christ. No matter what the
future holds, you will never be alone when Jesus lives within.

Humble yourselves before the Lord, and he will lift you up.

JAMES 4:10

JULY 3

How do we achieve [[sprititual]] renewal? First, there must
be prayer—the kind that springs from a deep-seated heart-yearning
for revival. We do not need pious platitudes and religious mouthings
—but earnest, fervent prayer.

Second, we Christians must forsake our sins, both individually
and corporately. We must forsake our pettiness, our peevishness,
our littleness, and our conflicts—as well as our evil ways.

Third, God must become real to us. Let the Bible's truth
soak deeply into your heart and mind every day.

O Lord, revive thy work in the midst of the years.
HABAKKUK 3:2 KJV

JUNE 29

Sometimes life brings us to the point where we don't see much hope for the future. If you're there right now—whatever the situation, whatever the reason—let me assure you that God cares, and because of Him your future can be different.

Committing our lives to Christ or renewing our commitment to Him doesn't mean all our problems will suddenly vanish. We can't undo the past, and when we have made unwise decisions, we often have to live with the consequences.

God loves you, and even when life is dark and uncertain, that truth will bring you encouragement and strength. Jesus knows what you are going through, and...He is praying for you.

[Jesus] is able to save completely those who come to God through him, because he always lives to intercede for them.

HEBREWS 7:25

JULY 2

Abraham Lincoln once said, "The strength of a nation
lies in the people—in the homes of the people."

I don't believe that young people today can live clean,
pure lives without the help of God. The peer pressure is too great,
and the temptations they see in the movies and on television,
and what they hear in their music is too much. Only Christ can
protect them. Only Christ can give them the power to say no.

Who in your home...in your neighborhood...in your life...would God have
you prayerfully and carefully teach His truth and His way? Start today.

*Teach [God's words] to your children, talking about them
when you sit at home and when you walk along the road,
when you lie down and when you get up.*

DEUTERONOMY 11:19

JUNE 30

Too many people today feel that the old moral standards are useless and out of date, and they ought to be free to make up their own minds about what is right and what is wrong.

I wonder if we have honestly faced the logical result of this belief. What is actually being said is that there is no such thing as right or wrong, and we should be free to decide how we want to behave. The moral standards God has given us are always best—for society, and for us as individuals. The reason is because He created us, He loves us, and He knows what is best for us.

Everyone did what was right in his own eyes.
JUDGES 21:25 NKJV

JULY 1

The Puritans were ready to order their personal life, worship, church, business affairs, political views, even recreation according to the Bible's commandments. What a contrast between the conduct of those earlier Christians and the permissiveness of our day!

Millions today want instant gratification. The whole world seems bent on pleasure, and there is an alarming preoccupation with self. When nations or individuals live only for pleasure, they begin to die morally and spiritually, oblivious to God's will and scornful of His judgment.

The Puritans knew that the life of faith is a struggle. Still they persevered in their faith. May it be said of us that our faith is "the business of [our] lives."

The proverbs of Solomon...for acquiring a disciplined and prudent life, doing what is right and just and fair.

PROVERBS 1:1, 3